The Costs of Regulation – and How the EU Makes Them Worse

by William Mason

© The Bruges Group 2008

Published in May 2008 by
The Bruges Group, 227 Linen Hall, 162-168 Regent Street, London W1B 5TB
www.brugesgroup.com

Bruges Group publications are not intended to represent a corporate view of European and international developments. Contributions are chosen on the basis of their intellectual rigour and their ability to open up new avenues for debate.

About the Author

William Mason lives in West Sussex with his wife and children. He is a Chichester District Councillor. He studied at Durham and Oxford. He first gained experience of the EU while working for an MEP during university holidays and has since added to that through work for multinational firms on three continents. As a former Special Constable and School Governor he has had firsthand experience of the inhibitions which excessive regulation has on the ability of volunteers and other workers to make a difference.

Table of Contents

EXECUTIVE SUMMARY

All societies require some regulation to protect people and the environment and to enhance economic efficiency. But, that fact acknowledged, there is great value to society in not regulating all aspects of life. There is an imbalance between those pushing for ever more intrusive regulation to reduce risk, and those who recognise the value of a free society. This imbalance leads to overregulation. While the supposed gains from any given piece of legislation are often well understood the negative costs for society rarely attract attention. Membership of the EU worsens this imbalance.

The government, including the EU, increasingly seeks to manage the risks that affect citizens as they pass through life. This is bad for society. Risk has a value, not just commercially, but also at an individual level. We have sleepwalked into an over-regulated society where communities are increasingly dysfunctional — the state, via regulation, is destroying a culture which valued self help, personal responsibility and community action.

Furthermore, this over-regulation leads many individuals to lead lives that are both greyer and more lacking in achievement and fulfilment than they should be. The modern social democratic state (as epitomised by both the current British government and by the EU institutions) is obsessed with reducing risk without regard to adverse consequences.

The state has a natural tendency towards control through regulation. Pressure groups, the media and the decline of civic society organisations such as the church have all encouraged ever - increasing regulation by the state and the EU. When either the state or the EU decide not to regulate, the likelihood is that the other will step into the perceived void – the risk of regulation of any given activity may be doubled through the UK's membership of the EU.

The new competencies that the EU will acquire under the Lisbon Treaty, which we are about to have imposed on us, will make the current situation with regard to the EU even worse and over-regulation even more likely. Unlike the nation state, the EU often seeks to regulate because its institutions see regulation as a necessary way of building a common European identity, irrespective of the costs.

This state-building motivation, together with the primacy the EU accords to the precautionary principle and the excuse which the poor quality legal framework in many former Warsaw Pact countries gives it to create more EU level regulation, amount to a recipe for over-regulation. Furthermore, the division of powers between the EU institutions makes it more likely that ill-conceived amendments will be made to EU regulations, whilst repealing and reforming those which clearly don't work is a task to make the best intentioned and most resolute European official quail.

Further to these difficulties, the compromises on which most EU laws are based (and that result from negotiations between different member states) ensure that the laws are often ambiguous. This causes problems for British civil servants and non-governmental organisations charged with implementing them; and in practice this often leads to over-implementation of EU regulations in the UK. The implementing legislation ends up restricting a free society in ways that those who originally drafted them in EU Commission directorates probably never intended. With these processes in place, freedom has little chance. Were this not enough, the EU's Charter of Fundamental Rights and Court of Justice are platforms for justifying yet more risk-reducing and freedom-inhibiting regulation, but are surprisingly weak when it comes to defending individual freedoms.

The resilience of society is not measured in pounds or even euros, so it is very difficult to calculate the cost that over-regulation of risk imposes on society. The measurable cost of regulation to businesses and charities is probably akin to £100 billion, with EU regulation accounting for around half the total. A reasonable case can be made that the intangible costs to society are even greater.

We need radical change if we are to create a healthier society where individuals and communities can thrive and live rather than merely exist as clients of the state or supra-state. Innovative solutions that would help reverse the regulatory imbalances are available to us. We must place more institutional hurdles in the way of regulations so that they are subject to more sceptical analysis prior to legislation. We need Whitehall to confine itself to regulating with respect to issues – such as clean air – with which it is best placed to deal, while leaving many others to local communities and the individual to manage.

The dynamic of the regulatory system can be fundamentally altered through a combination of measures including: educational improvement; healthcare reform; using alternatives to classic prescriptive regulation; using democracy to tame the media's lobbying for ever more regulation in the wake of each tragedy; litigation reform; equalising funding opportunities for holistic and single issue pressure groups; reducing the number of MPs and increasing the opportunities for ministers to manage government bodies rather than merely legislating.

All of the above reforms would help the UK create a freer and more harmonious society, more resilient and better able to help each individual achieve his or her potential – a worthy achievement for politicians on both the right and left of the political spectrum.

Of course, these vital reforms can't happen without a substantial renegotiation of the terms on which Britain participates in the European Union. Without that, the value of the reforms this paper advocates would be negated by legislation imposed on Britain by the EU institutions.

Good regulation is not easy. It will always be an art rather than a science but our leaders need to appreciate the probability that their quest for risk reduction has damaged and will continue to damage our culture and society. Politicians need to have the courage to implement radical changes if we are to survive as a free people.

Chapter 1

HOW REGULATION CAN DAMAGE SOCIETY

1.1 WHY REGULATION?

Life in the wilds, as Hobbes famously noted, is "solitary, poor, nasty, brutish, and short".[1] The remark provides the essential justification for regulation, namely that it allows societies to organise themselves, and individuals within them to live safely, create and trade. Regulation can protect people and the environment and promote economic efficiency.

Protecting People: Regulation, at its most basic, makes it more costly for people to attack one another. At a more sophisticated level, modern regulation such as the 1974 Health & Safety at Work Act can help reduce the risks of workplace accidents.

Economic Efficiency: Using money for trade is generally much more efficient than barter; and from ancient times, kings passed stringent laws laying down standards for coinage. In the modern world, many more aspects of commerce, such as company accounts, are regulated, so that information about a business can be inexpensively acquired, thus reducing the costs of investment.

Protecting the Environment: As industry develops, regulation advances beyond simple property rights. Air and water pollution is now regulated, and natural habitats protected from development. Such regulation can significantly increase the quality of life.

The section above sets out what regulation encompasses. Definitions of regulation are often unhelpfully technocratic. In this paper, regulation is defined as all forms of law and official guidance that regulate the conduct of individuals and organisations. The focus of the paper is the management of risk by the state.

1.2 THE CHALLENGE OF REGULATION

The case for regulation is self evident – but it does not imply that all regulation is good, or that everything should be regulated. This study argues that not having every aspect of our lives regulated is also valuable. It suggests that the EU worsens

---

1   Thomas Hobbes: *Leviathan* (1651) Part XIII

an imbalance between the forces pushing for more regulation and those that favour a free society.

Regulation is used to reduce risk, but a degree of risk in our lives is valuable; and at some point, the negative consequences of additional regulation outweigh the benefits that regulation is intended to deliver. Regulation that forced surgeons to use disposable scalpels to avoid any risk of CJD, for example, probably caused more people to suffer than it saved from suffering. Fewer people may have been harmed had surgeons continued to use higher quality reusable instruments, even if these carried a miniscule risk of infection.

Whether the adverse consequences of a regulation outweigh its benefits is, of course, a matter of judgment. This study, however, is not directly concerned with the location of that point. Rather, I seek to demonstrate that our regulatory culture is subject to bias. The supposed gains from any given piece of legislation are well understood, but the negative consequences, and particularly the unintended negative consequences, are rarely understood to the same degree. Moreover, the unintended negative consequences are always likely to be less well known. Hence, a rational government, seeking to benefit society, should reject regulation even when the evidence appears slightly favourable to it.[2] The risk that regulators seek to control has a value as well as a cost.

Chapter 2
Examples

Before turning to analysis, some examples of regulation in practice will help to define the issues. This chapter sets out some case studies which have been subject to intense scrutiny and critique.[3] There are probably more dramatic examples, and certainly examples with greater economic significance, but these cases illustrate the negative effect that regulation, intended to reduce risk, can have on the lives of people in all strata of society and all types of civic and charitable organisation.

---

2 It could be argued that there is a logical flaw in this case in that there will be unintended *positive* consequences as well. Policy makers, though, are generally far keener to make the case for a regulation than to find arguments against it. They are therefore far more likely to understand all possible benefits, and there will therefore, typically be fewer positive unintended consequences than negative ones.

3 Produced by the Government-funded Better Regulation Task Force and Better Regulation Commission.

2.1 CATHEDRAL CAMPS[4]

'Cathedral Camps' was a charity that gave young people the chance to work on historic buildings. The camps were held at cathedrals and churches throughout the UK, where volunteers could help to clean and maintain these sites. Often this involved being strapped into harnesses and climbing ladders to work on church spires and towers.

As new health and safety regulations were implemented, Cathedral Camps volunteers found their activities increasingly restricted. Finally, in an effort to reduce the risk of accidents the maintenance of towers and spires was restricted to professional steeplejacks. Volunteers were instead asked to carry out more mundane tasks.

Although no volunteers were ever injured in the Camps' twenty-five year history, insurance costs continued to escalate. In 2006, insurance costs were deemed to be so high as to preclude any further volunteer activities. Cathedral Camps was disbanded in the same year.

Issues

Were the associated insurance costs proportionate? As no volunteers were injured during these activities, what were the main factors driving up insurance premiums?

How else could the risks involved in Cathedral Camps activities have been managed? Who should have been held responsible for the risks involved?

If fit and healthy volunteers wish to spend their holiday maintaining churches and cathedrals, under what circumstances can they legitimately be prevented from doing so?

2.2 The Adventure Licensing Authority[5]

On 22 March 1993, four teenagers drowned whilst on a kayaking trip at Lyme Bay, off the Dorset coast, when their kayaks were swamped by high waves. The trip was organised by an outdoor centre which allocated two canoeing instructors to accompany the school party of eight teenagers and one teacher.

---

4   *Risk, Responsibility and Regulation – Whose Risk is it Anyway ?* (October 2006) Better Regulation Commission, p. 16

5   *Risk, Responsibility and Regulation – Whose Risk is it Anyway ?* (October 2006) Better Regulation Commission, p. 8

Although the party had been due to return from the trip at noon the emergency services were not called out until 3.30 pm, and the survivors were not rescued until later that evening. The subsequent trial resulted in the convictions of the owner of the activity centre and the centre itself on corporate manslaughter charges.

Prior to the Lyme Bay incident, providers of outdoor activities could opt in to a variety of voluntary codes of practice. However, the incident provoked an emotive campaign, led by the parents of the victims and supported by the press, the National Union of Teachers and some MPs. They pressed hard for tightened regulations on outdoor activity centres and for a statutory national system of accreditation and inspection.

Throughout this campaign the Health and Safety Executive (HSE) and the Government argued that legislation was unnecessary and supported a revised self-regulatory system. However, as a result of the campaign, the Activities Centres (Young Persons Safety) Act was implemented in 1995, which led to the creation of the Adventure Activities Licensing Authority (AALA). The regulations require all activity centres to apply for a licence and to be inspected by the AALA. Half of the estimated 1500 providers of adventure activities coaching applied for a licence. Only 13 of these had their applications refused.

Issues

Would the Lyme Bay tragedy have been avoided if the current system had been in place? Was the regulatory response proportionate to the risk implicit in participating in adventure activities? Who should take responsibility for that risk?

Not all adventure activities are covered by the Act. Why were other dangerous activities, such as horse riding, excluded?

Has the creation of the AALA resulted in the closure of activities centres? If so, what impact has this had on other related risks, such as childhood obesity?

2.3 New child car seats regulation[6]

A survey conducted by the Transport Research Laboratory in 2004 showed that 5% of 0-4 year olds were not restrained in any way when travelling in the rear of cars. In that year, 24 children aged 0-11 were killed in car accidents, 372 seriously injured, with 1,604 children estimated to have suffered light injuries.

6   *Ibid*, p. 10

Studies have shown that adult belts do not provide the best protection for a child. Changes to the law aim to substantially reduce the number of child injuries and fatalities caused by children without restraints or using unsuitable adult belts.

Earlier EC rules, required child seats and boosters to be used 'if available'. New EU child-seat regulations for cars came into force in the UK on 18 September 2006. Children up to the age of 12 and under 135cm are not allowed to travel unless they are in an approved safety seat (i.e. child seat or booster). Offenders can be fined a £30 fixed penalty or £500 if the case goes to court.

The new rules reflect advice that has been given for many years to those transporting children. Surveys show, however, that in spite of this advice, the vast majority of children over five travel in adult belts when they should be using a child seat, and that a significant minority are provided with no restraint at all. The appropriateness of child car seats depends on the weight of children. As a child's weight changes it is necessary for them to move up from one type of seat to another. To be equipped with appropriate seats for the age of their child, parents would need up to four car seats to ensure maximum safety (a rear-facing baby seat, a forward-facing child seat, a booster seat and a booster cushion designed for larger children over 22 kg).

The law allows for a few exceptions. It is recognised that it is impracticable to expect the right child seat or booster to be available in a taxi unless parents have brought one with them. "Short and occasional journeys" made for reasons of "unexpected necessity" are also exempted. This makes enforcement difficult for the police who were expected to "use common sense" by former Road Safety Minister Stephen Ladyman. He expected officers to appear at school gates from time to time to give parents advice.

Issues

Is it reasonable to expect parents to be able to comply with the rules? Is the state responsible for setting and enforcing rules for parents to transport their own young children?

Could parents occasionally refuse to carry another child if no adequate child seat is available? Might the law lead to other risks to children, such as leaving them to walk the streets unsupervised?

If enforcement of the law is not meant to be strict, would a non-regulatory approach such as a high-profile education campaign have reached the same outcome in a more efficient and proportionate manner?

2.4 School Lunchbox inspections[7]

Recent Government figures show that obesity levels among children are reaching unprecedented levels. Current trends indicate that by 2010, more than a million British children will be classed as obese. This means that obesity in girls is expected to rise from 16% to 22% by that time; for boys it is expected to increase to 19% (a rise of 2%).[8] Childhood obesity has been linked to medical problems in (young) adulthood including diabetes, heart problems and a range of cancers. Obesity is expensive for the NHS and for the national economy.

The public response

TV chef Jamie Oliver caused a media storm with his school dinners campaign that revealed that large numbers of children were eating low-quality junk food at school. Research commissioned by the Department for Education and Skills and the Food Standards Agency prompted the Government to commission the School Meals Review Panel to recommend changes to current school meal standards to reduce fat, salt and sugar.

The Panel's recommendations, which were implemented in the 2006/7 academic year, include:

* banning salt from dinner tables;

* increasing the quality of meat products, such as burgers, and reducing the frequency with which they are served; and

* restricting the serving of deep fried foods to twice a week.

As part of the drive to improve healthy eating in school, many schools have developed whole school food policies, which include rules on what foods can be brought onto school premises in lunchboxes. Food deemed to be unhealthy is sometimes removed and locked away until home-time. Schools set such policies in the context of their responsibility for various aspects of the day-to-day running of the school, such as conduct or school uniform. However, this has upset some of the children affected and brought objections from parents, who feel that schools should not be interfering in what they choose to give their children to eat.

---

7   *Risk, Responsibility and Regulation – Whose Risk is it Anyway ?* (October 2006) Better Regulation Commission, p. 28

8   *Forecasting Obesity to 2010,* Joint Health Survey's Unit, August 2006

Issues

Who should decide what food children can take into school: parents, schools or the Government?

How should the risk of increasing levels of childhood obesity be managed? Who is best placed to manage that risk?

How might the Government open up the broader debate to include relevant other policies such as those affecting the access of young people to sports and playing fields?

2.5 Dangerous Dogs Act 1991[9]

In the early 1990s, a spate of vicious dog attacks was widely reported in the national Press. The reports followed the death of an 11 year old child, killed in Scotland in 1989 by two Rottweilers. Public outcry followed a number of maulings of children by dogs and photographs of their often horrific injuries were presented across the front pages.

Mounting pressure on Parliament resulted in the Dangerous Dogs Act in 1991. The Act introduced strict guidelines for owners about how their dogs should behave in public. It also identified breeds of 'dangerous dogs' and targeted pit bull terriers and similar breeds.

Dogs deemed dangerous under the Act must be registered, micro-chipped, insured, muzzled and kept on a lead in public. The penalty for flouting the new law was harsh: owners could be ordered to pay hefty fines and could be imprisoned for up to two years. Unregistered dangerous breeds were mandatorily destroyed.

Following a backlash from dog owners and widely-reported cases of unregistered cross breeds being destroyed, the Act was amended in 1997. The mandatory death penalty on unregistered dogs was dropped.

Hard statistics of the incidence of dog attacks in the UK are not publicly available, but "what figures exist suggest that deaths from dog attack are in single figures each year ... and the biggest risk of dog attack appears to be in the home from the family pet".

Figures are available for 2001, when 3400 people were hospitalised after dog attacks. This figure, 10 years after the Act's implementation, showed a 25%

9 *Risk, Responsibility and Regulation – Whose Risk is it Anyway?* (October 2006) Better Regulation Commission, p. 22

increase in dog attacks between 1996 and 2001. In September 2006, two horrific attacks on children by Rottweilers — not a breeds covered by the 1991 Act — hit the headlines.

Issues

Has the Act achieved its objectives? Was regulation the best way to deal with the risk of attack by dangerous dogs?

One school of thought suggests that a dog's behaviour is strongly influenced by the way it is brought up and trained. Was the Act correctly targeted?

It is often difficult to distinguish banned breeds or to determine whether cross-breeds are deemed dangerous. Could a different approach have made enforcement easier?

2.6 Hatfield Rail Crash[10]

On 17 October, 2000, a high speed passenger train bound for Leeds derailed at Hatfield in Hertfordshire. The train had been travelling at over 115mph. Of the 200 passengers on board, 4 were killed and 70 injured. Subsequent investigations found that microscopic cracks in the rails caused a rail to fragment when the train passed over it at high speed.

Railtrack, which at the time owned all rail tracks across Britain, imposed speed restrictions across many miles of railway while investigators assessed the safety of the tracks. Railtrack acted to avoid the risk of further accidents and subsequent personal injury claims. The speed restrictions, some of which were as low as 20mph, caused massive disruption across the network for around a year after the crash.

There is no doubt that Railtrack acted in a way they believed would best protect the health and safety of rail passengers. The widespread disruption of rail travel, however, led many commuters to travel by car instead of rail. But the risk of dying on the roads is greater than that of travelling by rail: it has been estimated that "the increase in automobile traffic led to five additional [road] deaths in the first thirty days after the Hatfield crash".[11]

---

10 *Risk, Responsibility and Regulation – Whose Risk is it Anyway ?* (October 2006) Better Regulation Commission, p.36

11 Sunstein: *Risk and Reason,* p. 2

Issues

Was Railtrack's response to the crash proportionate? Should Railtrack have considered the wider safety implications of its decision to reduce speed limits on the railways? What role might the Government have played in this?

2.7 Carers Sitter Service[12]

The CSS is a small charity providing respite services for carers of older people. But because tasks like helping someone out of a chair to go to the bathroom are classified as 'personal care', the charity was told it needed to register as a 'provider of personal care', which broght it within the scope of the Domiciliary Care National Minimum Standards. This meant that volunteers would have to undertake NVQ training, amongst other things, to continue helping those in need. The charity reluctantly decided to withdraw its personal care assistance –– a change that benefited no one.

The Better Regulation Task Force encouraged the CSS to re-contact the Commission for Social Care Inspection. CSCI agreed to help to find a solution. In order to apply a proportionate approach and deal more sensitively with such cases, CSCI met with CSS, listened to their views and the details of the service they delivered. The complex case took several months to resolve. However a solution was arrived at, which involved taking a proposal to the commission for endorsement of a policy change that would apply to all voluntary services. By registering the CSS as an Introductory Employment Agency (an agency that solely acts as introducers of workers employed by the user) rather than as a Domiciliary Care Agency, the CSS was able to continue providing its valuable service in its current form.

2.8 Playbus[13]

Community Links, founded in 1977, is an innovative inner-city charity running community-based projects in east London. It helps over 50,000 vulnerable children, young people and adults every year. Its work has influenced community-based organisations nationwide and government policy. Eighty percent of its staff live in east London and many of these are former users of its services. One of Community Links' first ventures was a play bus that travelled around Newham providing recreational facilities to communities that often did not have them.

12 *Better Regulation for Civil Society – Making life easier for those who help others* (November 2005) Better Regulation Task Force, p. 20

13 *Better Regulation for Civil Society – Making life easier for those who help others* (November 2005) Better Regulation Task Force, p. 21

However, the charity believes that many of their early schemes, such as the playbus, would be considerably more difficult to set up in today's regulatory environment. The playbus scheme, for example, would be subject to health and safety regulations, Ofsted inspections, CRB checks for workers and training for people working with children. Whilst the protection of children has to be paramount, it is also important that regulation does not squash innovative schemes in disadvantaged communities before they have even started.

2.9 Women Acting in Today's Society[14]

Women Acting In Today's Society (WAITS) is a women's educational trust that supports women from a wide range of educational, social and cultural backgrounds to address issues such as welfare benefits, social education, domestic violence, isolation, health and crime; and provides skills such as confidence-building, assertiveness, community profiling and public speaking. Often WAITS works with women from deprived areas and most project staff and volunteers have personal experience of the issues facing women who suffer from domestic violence. Many became involved with WAITS as service users or volunteers, and all have personal experience of living or working with black and minority ethnic groups.

One member of WAITS staff was working with a client who was suffering from domestic violence. When the client's child became implicated in the violence, social services requested a child-case conference. The WAITS worker wanted to represent her client at the case conference, as she had built up a strong relationship with the woman and understood her complex situation. However, the local authority specified that only a parent or a social services worker could act as a representative at the case conference. A social services worker, though, would have had no prior understanding of the woman's difficult situation and may not have been able to serve the client as effectively or sensitively as the WAITS worker.

Voluntary sector workers should be able to represent their clients where the client requests it. Neither regulation nor over-interpretation of regulation should lead to decreased levels of support for vulnerable people.

---

14 *Better Regulation for Civil Society – Making life easier for those who help others* (November 2005) Better Regulation Task Force, p. 38

2.10 Learning and Skills Council[15]

In mid-2003, a London voluntary organisation (the Organisation) was awarded a grant of just over £200,000 from the London Learning and Skills Council (LSC). The amount awarded contributing to an overall operational budget of £350,000 for a period of 15 months. The project offered support to small VCOs with little or no access to support and advice, and umbrella organisations with a coordinating and supporting role to other organisations.

Reporting / Monitoring Requirements

The LSC required monthly narrative reports that compared the delivery plan with the outcomes, outputs, and milestones achieved. It required an explanation of any deviations and evaluation of the project to date. There were also electronic reporting requirements; two evaluation reports (one intermediate and one final); one control environment questionnaire explaining the systems employed for managing the project; maintenance of the delivery plan Excel workbook used by LSC (which listed all the outputs profiled and the associated unit costs); quarterly visits from the LSC contract manager and an auditor's visit; a paper trail verifying eligibility for each organisation supported by the programme and other evidence for expenditure, i.e. advertisements for posts, etc.

Issues

- Contracts were not signed until three months into the project creating a backlog in reporting and collating physical evidence. In addition, guidance notes were delayed.

- The LSC contract manager did not communicate the requirements for evidence clearly to the Organisation's project manager. There was a poor understanding by the LSC contract manager and the Organisation on the systems needed to manage such projects. This delayed gathering information for evidence and monitoring requirements effectively and consistently.

The Organisation agreed with the LSC that it would use its own registration forms (for the smaller organisations the Organisation was contracted to provide services to). However, later, all forms for a six-month period had to be redone as they did not have the European Social Fund or LSC logo. The Organisation couldn't see how this inhibited the project, since the logos were on all promotional materials, which

---

15 *Better Regulation for Civil Society – Making life easier for those who help others* (November 2005) Better Regulation Task Force, p. 54

is what the guidelines required. In addition, the registration forms will continue to be used by the Organisation well after the end of the programme, regardless of the current funder(s).

- The Excel workbook provided by the LSC was susceptible to error during handling because the formulas and references are not protected. This can offset formulas causing erroneous calculations. This meant spending time tracking down the error, or starting again with a new workbook.

- The on-line system was not reliable, and the interface was not user friendly. Furthermore, the information entered online simply duplicated the narrative reports so the Organisation had to report the same thing twice. In the end problems led to the online system being abandoned.

- Verifying eligibility for the support the Organisation was offering (i.e. approx. <£28 million annual income, and <250 staff for the VCO being advised) via its advice line was impossible, as it required a representative from the Organisation to verify the information collected, which was not feasible. Furthermore, the eligibility criteria covered all the VCOs the Organisation worked with. The Organisation had to negotiate constantly about this, especially after the auditors threatened to claw back some of the money.

- Overall, the monitoring requirements seemed onerous for a relatively small organisation, and the value of gathering the information was unclear.

2.11 The Community Foundation for Northern Ireland[16]

The Community Foundation for Northern Ireland works to support people, strengthen communities and build peace in the divided communities of Northern Ireland. The Community Foundation for Northern Ireland's mission is to improve the quality of life through enabling communities to tackle social need and divisions by funding and supporting community-based action, raising funds, suggesting policy and producing publications. The Community Foundation, at the request of the Department for Social Development, was managing a two year Local Development Fund for the Department. This was intended to deliver a £1m per annum grant to specific 'low community infrastructure' areas of Belfast.

In addition to a 41 page Operations Manual, there were some 13 forms that had to be potentially completed by the Community Foundation in order to enable

16 *Better Regulation for Civil Society – Making life easier for those who help others* (November 2005) Better Regulation Task Force, p. 58

applicant groups to access the available funds. These included an application form (13 pages), activity outputs and outcomes form, duplication funding checklist, assessment form, financial plan form, technical assistance costs form (and apportionment), variations pro forma confirmation of expenditure verification form, document summary sheet, quarterly progress report form, post project evaluation report and completion of lessons learnt report.

In addition to negotiating a consensual community approach (which can be difficult and time consuming in fragmented and divided areas) the Foundation had to complete all the forms involved for each grant. The technical assistance budget available to support this work was set at 5% (some £50,000 per annum). Consequently the Foundation was faced with subsidising the cost of delivering a departmental programme. This excessively bureaucratic approach is audit driven – a drive that often undermines the real purpose of grants.

The emphasis on overly-rigid audit comes from the experience of the implementation of the European Union Peace Programmes in Northern Ireland. A recent example of the latter is where a Community Foundation worker had to drive around a number of projects in an attempt to find receipts for some £5,000 for exhibition display equipment that had been purchased with grant funding in 1996 – the audit which demanded the original invoices/receipts was carried out in July 2003. In 2005, the Department for Social Development was still seeking the receipts. No one can argue with the need to be accountable, but such lack of flexibility can only damage service delivery.

2.12 CESSAHA[17][18]

CESSAHA operates a charitable housing association providing sheltered housing for older ex-service men and women, as well as a registered charity that offers cafes and shops for active service personnel and their dependants in the UK and Sovereign Bases in Cyprus. Some of the recent changes to regulations that it has faced, and its comments on the effects of these, are listed below.

1. **The Housing Corporation Regulatory and Statistical Return:** ever changing format.

---

17 CESSAHA stands for Church of England Soldiers', Sailors' and Airmen's Housing Association Ltd

18 *Better Regulation for Civil Society – Making life easier for those who help others* (November 2005) Better Regulation Task Force, p. 17

2. **Best Value:** would have cost more to analyse than could ever be saved. This was a bureaucratic approach to running a business sensibly; fortunately it seems to have lost favour.

3. **Performance Standards:** more paper and returns.

4. **Tenant Participation:** a good principle but do 80-year old sheltered housing tenants really want to sit on Health and Safety Committees?

5. **Supporting People:** very bureaucratic - the requirements are not realistic for the elderly.

6. **Health and Safety Risk Assessment:** good basic principles are overwhelmed by the bureaucratic requirement of reams of safety documents for items that are kept under every domestic sink in the country.

7. **Fire Risk Assessment:** unloads fire brigades' costs onto charity.

8. **Financial Risk Assessment:** not bad but basically just common sense.

9. **Housing Benefit Applications:** "Dire for an eighty year old."

10. **Rent Restructuring:** calls for above-inflation rent increases with lower pension rises for the elderly. They refused to comply and declared this to the Housing Corporation.

11. **Criminal Records Bureau:** chaotic admin and spiralling costs for users.

12. **Charity Commission Summary Information Return:** considerable extra work with no benefits for those who do not seek bequests.

13. **Training Agency Returns:** more data collection for government.

14. **Revised electrical installation regulations:** can no longer use own ex-RN maintenance staff even though they are I.E.E. qualified.

15. **Data Protection Act registration:** now annual instead of triennial bureaucracy, more costs.

16. **Housing Efficiency Returns:** out of touch with reality; punishment for the already efficient, unclear requirements.

17. **NROSH** - Housing database project: no notice of extra workload, more costs for us; assumption of surplus IT staff or extensive database knowledge.

18. **Local Authority Business Alliances:** devoid of understanding of small businesses.

19. **Housing Corporation Added Value study**: no notice, short return time.

20. **New Tax Return:** HM Revenue & Customs prefer this in a complex IT format.

21. **Decent Homes Standard:** good principle buried by bureaucracy.

22. **SORP:** ever increasing requirements; more work.

23. **Government Web Sites:** the following public bodies appear to assume we have time to search websites hoping to prevent penalties for not finding and complying with new legislation announced online only to save costs:

   - The Housing Corporation

   - Charity Commission

   - Office of Deputy Prime Minister

   - Health & Safety Executive

   - Audit Commission

   - Department of Work and Pensions

   - Department of Trade and Industry

2.13 EUROPEAN REGULATION

The examples above come about as a result of a mixture of British and European regulation. The specific problems of European regulation can be illustrated by looking at just one narrow area – food labelling – where the EU is keen on regulation.

For a start, regulation is inconsistent:

Example: Where a certain ingredient is emphasised on the packaging of olive oil for marketing purposes, EU law requires the quantity of that ingredient to be indicated. The producer can indicate this information either directly after the product description or in the ingredients panel. In practice, most retailers include the information in the ingredients panel.

However, the EU regulation on olive oil marketing standards obliges food manufacturers who want to highlight olive oil to label the quantity of oil used directly after the product description.[19] This inconsistency between

19 Commission Regulation (EC) no. 1019/2002

23

Directives can mean that consumers are faced with, for example, choosing a pizza and finding information about the quantity of tomatoes and ham on the ingredient label, and then having to refer to the product description to find the same information on olive oil.[20]

Then there is simple overregulation:

Example: The Scotch Whisky Association has identified more than a dozen different EU Directives and Regulations which have a bearing on the labelling of alcoholic drinks.[21]

Regulation is also inept:

Example: The legal framework for nutritional information, where it is provided, currently requires sodium to be declared. However the term "sodium" does not represent the salt content of a product, e.g. 6 grams of salt a day represents only about 2.5g of sodium. Adults are recommended to consume around 6 grams of salt per day. It makes little sense to advise consumers using one term but to label using another.[22]

None of the above is surprising considering how poorly the Commission sometimes consults:

Example: The Commission-sponsored report into food labelling was supported by consumer research involving interviews with only 90 individuals. Such research, claimed to have been carried out in "London suburbs and Birmingham, Paris suburbs and Montpellier and Rome suburbs and Turin" could not have been representative of the views of European Union consumers.[23]

It would be nice to think that food labelling was an aberration but, sadly, there is poor regulation in other areas. Sometimes the competitive disadvantages imposed by regulations appear to be ignored:

Example: Changes to the Television Without Frontiers Directive[24] are being proposed to extend the directive to internet regulation. It appears

---

20 *Make it Simple, Make it Better* (Dec 2004) Better Regulation Task Force, p. 35

21 *Ibid*, p. 35

22 *Ibid*, p. 37

23 *Ibid*, p. 41

24 Directive 89/552/EEC

that certain outcomes, such as the regulation of advertising and a right of reply, will be prescribed in the Directive itself. Website operators based outside the EU, however, will not be subject to these rules, whereas EU-based operators will be.

Website operators, though, unlike television broadcasters, are global in their reach. Some fear that European businesses will move to non-European bases to circumvent the requirements.[25]

Sometimes, the Commission's urge to jump to the most regulatory solution possible (the most integrative) is apparent:

Example: A number of significant electricity supply interruptions occurred around the world in the late summer of 2003, including in North East America and Eastern Canada, parts of London, eastern Denmark and Southern Sweden. Almost all of Italy was blacked out for nearly 24 hours in late September. The Commission reacted swiftly by announcing in December 2003 a proposal for a new regulation that was, among other things, intended to prevent future blackouts. The Commission, though, seems not to have thoroughly considered the option of 'no action'. The problem may have been better dealt with by individual Member States or by an amendment to the existing EU Electricity Directive, which already contains provisions about the security and supply of electricity.[26]

And then, of course there is the plain incompetent:

Example: Consultation on the Commission's proposal for a Directive on an Annual Corporate Governance Statement and Other Disclosure failed to meet the minimum standards. The Commission issued its consultation in April 2004, just six months before it adopted the formal proposal in October. The tight timetable meant the Commission allowed only six weeks for responses. The consultation was described by stakeholders as rushed and slapdash.[27]

As the following chapters argue, reforming EU regulation is not an ancillary topic which can be ignored in a discussion of regulation. Any cogent plan to restore some measure of freedom and liberty to our shores must address it.

---

25 *Routes to Better Regulation – A Guide to Alternatives to Classic Regulation* (Dec 2005) Better Regulation Task Force, p. 16

26 *Ibid*, p. 21

27 *Get Connected – Effective Engagement in the EU* (Sept 2005) Better Regulation Task Force, p. 37

Chapter 3
THE VALUE OF RISK

I recently spoke to the head of a large charity caring for adults with disabilities. She told me that the regulations, as enforced by the social care regulators, have been successful in driving risk out of the lives of the individuals for whom her organisation cares. She projected a slide onto the wall with a picture of a man sitting and writing his diary for a typical day. The entry read, "Dear diary...." and stopped. It stopped because there was nothing for him to write. Along with removing all risk from his existence, regulations have removed all reward from his life because they inhibit any activity that he might find fulfilling. When we get up in the morning and leave our houses, we take risks. But taking these risks allows us to do things with our lives, to play a part in society and to achieve some measure of fulfilment.

From a commercial perspective, taking risks can, correctly judged, lead to immense rewards. Boeing famously risked more money that the company was worth on development of the 747 Jumbo Jet. Its reward was domination of the civil aviation market for a generation. On a smaller scale, as discussed later, the same risk/reward dynamic applies to the communities and individuals that make up society.

There is a compelling case for regulating some aspects of some activities that we might, left to our own devices, undertake. What I argue in this chapter is that our current regulatory culture fails to take into account properly the less tangible and even intangible costs of regulation (such as the grey lives it imposes on adults with learning difficulties).

Current regulatory culture threatens our communities. Policy makers need to adopt different assumptions if they wish to avoid their regulations wounding those whom they seek to serve.

As the examples in the last chapter illustrate, the problem addressed in this chapter is not a hypothetical risk of overregulation damaging society but the here and now of British society. Even our own former Prime Minister, Mr Blair, cited Julia Neuberger's claim that if an old person falls to the floor, regulations decree that care workers cannot help them to their feet but must instead go and find a hoist before they can do so.[28] The Better Regulation Task Force said that more than a quarter of all working time in charities that work with the elderly is spent dealing with requests from

---

28 In a speech to the IPPR, May 2005, citing Baroness Neuberger's book *The Moral State We're In* (2005)

regulators[29] – time that might be better spent supporting elderly people. Similarly, 61% of a sample of welfare-focused charities surveyed believe that regulation was harming innovation in their charities.[30]

3.1 UNDERLYING CAUSES OF THE OVER-PROTECTIVE STATE

There are several causes underlying the growth of regulation designed to reduce the risks that regulators trust the individual to manage.

3.1.1 Natural Tendency of the State Towards Control and Regulation

It is natural for civil servants in Brussels and Whitehall to wish to exercise some influence over the policy areas in which they are expert. For the policy-making civil servant there must seem little point in becoming an expert if the acquired expertise can never be used to change anything. Of course, influence can be exercised in ways other than regulation, but regulation has become the default option for Whitehall because it feels more tangible to the bureaucrat than many other options.

EU bureaucrats are likely to be even worse in this respect than British ones. For them, regulation is the *raison d'être* – the primary means of ensuring greater integration within the EU. Laissez-faire and alternatives to classic regulation – such as education/awareness raising – take far longer to be effective than the two to three years most policy makers spend in each role.

If this observation can be made of the permanent civil services, similar traits can be seen in ministers and European Commissioners. The average junior minister, unlike the average civil servant, spends twenty years moving up the greasy pole and, having finally caught the PM's eye, wants to make an impression. He or she knows that it is necessary to make that impression quickly, to gain a profile with the media, impress those that count within the government, and to move further up the political ladder.

It is often said that the easiest way for a civil servant to get promoted is to serve on a bill team. The same may be said of a minister. What better way to prove his or her mettle than to take a controversial bill through a hostile House of Commons? This may perhaps be too cynical an explanation of ministerial-led regulation. Many politicians are in politics because they are passionate about issues and have spent many years developing ideas about how to improve society. Once in power, they

29 *Better Regulation for Civil Society* – BRTF – Nov 2005, p. 71

30 *Ibid*, p. 73

feel compelled to do something with their ideas as quickly as possible to give some meaning to the years they have spent in the political wilderness prior to arriving in Whitehall. All too often, a new piece of statute appeals as their way of making their contribution to British public life, even though its unintended consequences may severely damage the ideals they came into politics to serve.

This tendency is exacerbated by the restrictions placed on British law making by the EU. All too often a minister will find that the law he or she really wished to reform is untouchable – power having emigrated to the European Commission. The minister, in frustration, turns to making second-rate legislation – often in the form of regulations – which, a quarter of a century before, his or her predecessor, concerned with greater matters, would never have stooped to. The result is that we create a country which is, at once, more risk adverse and less free.

3.1.2 Role of the Media

The media also influences the political dynamic for regulation. Modern twenty-four-hour journalism puts great pressure on journalists to find stories. Disaster and personal tragedy, together with suitably gory or heart rending pictures are now piped into most sitting rooms on demand. For many people who don't naturally turn to the *Financial Times* or *The Economist* for information, this is the world as it is. It seems horrible, upsetting and in need of improvement; i.e. new regulation. Many politicians perceive this attitude to be widespread and to be reflected by the media. Meanwhile the media is keen to maintain its influence by masquerading as *vox populi*. Such perceived pressure leads politicians to respond by promising what they believe the public want to hear – promising that an accident or piece of maladministration will never happen again because of the new regulations that address the risk. Those advising them may know very well that no regulation will ever deliver on such promises but this does not stop the regulation becoming a reality.

3.1.3 The European Union

Were this domestic pressure not already sufficient, as a member state of the European Union, the UK has other legislative pressures put on it because of the European Commission's power to propose legislation. Many of the same pressures which bear on the British Civil Service bear upon their counterparts in the European Commission and, with much duplication between the EU and British policy making functions, there is an increased probability that either the British Civil Service or the European Commission will propose a new regulation to tackle a perceived risk, which might well be better left untreated by central government or supra-national regulation.

3.2 FAILURE OF SOCIETY TO PUSH BACK

Faced with the regulatory pressures outlined above, society does little to push back because the mechanisms which might have weakened historically the regulatory impulse have declined while other forces with a tendency to favour regulatory solutions have gained authority.

3.2.1 Pressure Groups

Political parties in the UK, which take a holistic view of the sort of society they want to see and the level of regulation appropriate to achieve it, have seen their membership haemorrhaging since the 1950s. One reason for this is that much of the politically-active population has found membership of single-issue pressure groups a more fulfilling way of achieving their objectives.

Pressure groups have far less interest in considering the adverse consequences of using a regulatory solution to address a risk they perceive to be dangerous. Many pressure groups enjoy charitable status and hence tax breaks (which political parties don't) and they can raise money more easily than parties. Through sustained long term campaigning on a specific issue they can achieve regulatory change (often increased regulation of risks which they are concerned about) through persistent reapplication to different combinations of civil servants and ministers over a number of years. In addition, even if Whitehall manages to be consistently hostile to change, the pressure groups have a further bite at the regulatory cherry through lobbying of European Commission bureaucrats and MEPs, who can impose change on the UK.

The pressure groups' regulatory proposals are not necessarily bad. But their consistent passion on a single issue may ensure a more regulated outcome than an erudite arbiter would arrive at after disinterestedly considering the merits of central (rather than local or individual) management of a specific risk.

One theory of government would have it that the supplanting of holistic political parties by pressure groups does not matter because pressure groups compete with one another – merely externalising what was previously debated within Whitehall departments and political parties. In some cases this happens - on issues such as nuclear power and animal testing where large and well organised pressure groups operate on each side - perhaps cancelling out each other's influence. In other areas, the outcomes are less benign as the UK Alliance for Childhood observes in its critique of what society's risk aversion is doing to childhood: "This latest expansion of vetting is little short of state regulation of all adult-child relations outside the home. Its corrosive effect on society in the long term, through fuelling a breakdown in contact and trust between the generations, could be incalculable."[31]

3.2.2 Organised Religion

A further reason for the inability of the society to resist regulation is the decline in organised religion. It may seem strange to associate the decline of religion in Western Europe with an increase in regulation. Yet Christianity, a faith with a strong belief in life after death, has historically been at the heart of Western culture and it is a key factor in understanding the increasing regulation of risk by the state.

First, if, as was historically the case, much of the local population believed that the local vicar and his acolytes were managing social and caring services on behalf of the village according to the teachings of the Church, there was little pressure for the state to regulate how social issues should be managed. In fact, the evidence suggests that a devout population was capable of resisting central social regulation as the Nazi party found out when it tried to impose its eugenics regulations on Catholics in Westphalia and Bavaria in 1941.[32] The decline in organised religion and the associated decline in confidence in the priesthood to oversee the provision of social and caring services has led many to look to the state for leadership and regulatory instructions on how to manage risk in such areas.

Second, on a more theological note, if one believes that the toils and tribulations of this world are merely a preparation for the next and, to quote J.K. Rowling's Professor Dumbledore, "After all, to the well-organised mind, death is but the next great adventure",[33] it is far easier to accept failings in our earthly life. Conversely, if one believes that death is an absolute then a humanistic moral imperative drives one to attempt to create Augustine's *Civitas Dei* in the *civitas terrena*. To put this more crudely, atheism or even agnosticism is likely to increase regulatory pressure, all other factors remaining constant. This tendency is exacerbated by the fact that

---

31 Tim Gill from his article on the adverse consequences of the reduction of risk in childhood in the Royal Society of Arts Journal April 2007 - http://www.thersa.org/journal/article.asp?articleID=1006

32 The Bishop of Munster, Clemens August Graf von Galen led the revolt again the Nazi T4 Eugenics programme with a public sermon on 3rd August 1941. This led to Hitler being jeered by an angry crowd at Hof near Nuremberg in August 1941. Hitler subsequently cancelled the Eugenics programme on 24th August 1941.

33 J.K. Rowling: *Harry Potter and the Philosopher's Stone,* Bloomsbury (1997), p. 215

many atheists have been attracted to the Marxism as an alternative code for life. Marxist dialectical materialism, of course, seeks to put the regulatory state at the heart of society as the solution to its ills.

Thus a decline in confidence in the precepts of the Christian faith as a regulatory code for life and individual risk management led a new political class to search for a different way to manage risks in society based on the centrality of the state as the guarantor of rational scientific policy making. There is nothing intrinsically wrong with rational scientific policy making by the state, when it is achieved, but it is intrinsically more likely to see regulation as the solution to the risks the individual faces than the self help, community help, education, tolerance of imperfect outcomes and prayer historically inspired by many Christian denominations.[34]

3.2.3 Boiled Frog Syndrome

A further explanation for the general acceptance of regulation is what might be described as the boiled frog syndrome. This refers to the well-known theory that when a frog is put into boiling water, it senses the heat and jumps out. But if a frog is put into cold water and the water slowly heated, the frog will remain in the water and boils to death.

This is a pertinent analogy for what has been happening to us as citizens over the past seventy years. Any one regulation may have negligible downside risks, but the cumulative effect of hundreds of regulations to eliminate related risks is much greater. The water becomes too hot to sustain life comfortably but, by that point, the nervous system, which should reject this approach to risk, is debilitated and cannot find a way out. This may be the state we currently find ourselves in and it certainly matches the reaction of many businesses I have spoken to about regulation. They dislike the whole but find it very difficult to find the specific regulation that could be repealed. This may be, in part, because of a declining appetite for risk but it may

---

34 It may seem odd to talk about the decline of religion in rural areas in the context of an predominantly urban British state in the 20th Century but its decline within the ruling class has happened within a short lifetime. Up until 1945 the House of Commons, and to an even greater extent the House of Lords contained a large number, if not a preponderance of aristocracy and gentry. While England had become a highly urban country a large number of Conservative MPs (the backbone of Parliament until Atlee's appointment as Prime Minister in 1945) had undergone a rural socialisation process. They grew up with the informal norms of rural society where the vicar and the squire had considerable influence on many aspects of village life. That urban life had been very different from this model for 150 years did not influence Parliament as much as it might. Commerce and industry - with its systems, processes and methods - was not only disliked by the left of the political spectrum for what it was perceived to do to workers but by many who sat in Parliament who, while reluctantly accepting the need for commerce, were guided in social policy by the diverse and informal risk management structures of the countryside.

also be due to a loss of institutional memory as to the workings of the informal and diverse methods used to handle a risk before the regulation was introduced.

Another underlying problem has been a general acceptance that the Whig view of history – that it is a ladder of progress though which the world and society inexorably becomes better and better – applies to regulation. We have become used to huge scientific advances enabling things utterly impossible for a previous generation and this normalisation of the extraordinary may have given rise to a belief that trade-offs do not have to be made when it comes to regulating to reduce risk.

The adverse consequences of using regulation to manage risk for the individual were not immediately apparent and risk removal has been treated as a free good. As we are all taught, gift horses should never be looked in the mouth. Had society understood that the regulatory horse had a great ability to bite the hand that fed it, society might have been more cautious.

To take a close analogy – in the post-war years the establishment in the West was obsessed (to a greater or lesser extent depending on the party in power) with fighting the Cold War. Many think tanks, such as the Institute for Economic Affairs, dedicated much energy to demonstrating the evils of excessive economic regulation of profit, wealth and so forth. In part, this energy was applied because the horse of state economic ownership and management was known to trot to the Gulag Archipelago or onto Chairman Mao's Cultural Revolution. Because the dangers of using regulation to manage individual risk have been less clear, resistance has been less well organised leading to regulation being used as the semi-automatic response to many risks.

3.3 ADVERSE CONSEQUENCES OF OVER-REGULATION

3.3.1 Inadvertently Increasing Risk

Over-regulation may actually increase risk. By failing to take a holistic view of regulation, a nuclear safety inspectorate might reduce the risk of one type of accident where the risk of an accident was already of the order of one in a billion while increasingly the likelihood of another type of accident with a risk of one in ten thousand. Over-regulation can be problematic because if an inspectorate or department is highly prescriptive in a narrow area it may be unable to appreciate the adverse consequences elsewhere.

Over-regulation also helps create a climate where many rewarding ideas and actions are explicitly banned by regulation. Even if not expressly banned, they may be deterred by a climate of pervasive state dependency. Those who would otherwise be active in society divert their energies into private spheres for fear that they will be pilloried for failing to follow some arcane health and safety regulation; or out of frustration at the necessity, if anything is to be achieved within the regulatory structure, of ploughing through a mountain of bureaucratic rules. The ability of community leaders to respond spontaneously and creatively is being lost.

As the OECD's chief regulatory economist put it, it is possible to put a premium on a society which is resilient, self reliant and innovative.[35] Over-regulation threatens these attributes. In their place, regulation is creating a culture that idealises victims rather than self help.

In innovative societies, people are free to take many different types of risk in pursuit of reward. In such permissive societies, for example, England in the century and a half that followed the restoration of Charles II and the later Glorious Revolution, some of the greatest advances have been made.

Conversely, Imperial China under the Ming and Qing dynasties was successful in maintaining a single authority for centuries. But the deliberate suppression of independent thought and local experiment (e.g. the ability to make individual risk judgments) that came with that achievement led to the decline of a civilisation that had previously surpassed Western Europe in wealth and sophistication.[36]

3.3.2 Lack of Personal Responsibility

Self-reliance is closely linked to personal responsibility. Tony Blair, when Prime Minister, indicated[37] that people need to take responsibility for their own actions. Taking responsibility involves assessing the risk in situations we are called upon to handle, making a judgment, and living with the consequences. Over-regulation and a culture of individual risk mitigation by the state through regulation threatens personal responsibility. I am not speaking here of the regulation the state makes to limit air pollution but rather, for example, the regulation it makes telling us how we must go about buying and selling our houses.[38] By giving us the impression that it is

35   Josef Konvitz – 7 December 2005

36   Dr John Kay, Former Chairman of London Business School – September 2003

37   Speech to IPPR – May 2005

38   Through Home Information Packs (HIPS)

always on the lookout for us, the state gives a false sense of security that supplants the natural instinct of *caveat emptor.* Thus we find ourselves drifting towards a situation where a large proportion of the population believe that something must be safe because no regulation says they cannot do it.

Pensions regulation encourages people to do the wrong thing and not to take individual responsibility. As the Turner Commission on pensions stated, overly-complex means-tested regulation designed to look after the poorest pensioners in society has the undesirable effect of discouraging personal responsibility by penalising individual saving to provide for old age.[39] Regulations governing the risks we are exposed to in our lives, passed with good intentions, have the effect of damaging personal responsibility.

Regulation surrounding how the children of single mothers are to be treated and cared for is problematic in that it has, in seeking to solve problems of deprivation, created multiple incentives for individuals to behave in ways which are likely to be costly for society. While these regulations are intended to protect the child from harm, they have negative effects, as Dame Butler-Sloss pointed out[40] in her speech to the Bar Council, "There is now no incentive to marry or remain married and a financial incentive to co-habit and not to marry." Thus single parenting, with all the disadvantages and dependency empirical evidence suggests it brings is encouraged and the ability of individuals to form bonds with one another to take responsibility for their own children reduced.

3.3.3 Damage to Communities

An obvious response to the charge that regulation produces declining personal responsibility is, "So what? Why does it matter?" It matters because without personal responsibility it is difficult, even unproductive, to have a community. If members of society have no shared standards of personal responsibility, how is it possible to enter transactions on any basis but distrust – that everyone outside the family – and possibly even within the family – is out to get you?

A walk around almost any town centre on an evening illustrates the lack of responsibility prevalent amongst some sections of society. This lack of responsibility, caused to a large extent by the regulatory state's near-fatal wounding of civil society is, to a great degree, self-reinforcing. The lack of shared norms of

---

39 *A New Pension Settlement for the Twenty-First Century - The Second Report of the Pensions Commission,* p. ix

40 Speech to the Bar Council 6th December 2005

social responsibility increases the expectation of individuals that the state will deal with their issues – victimhood rather than self-help becomes the norm.

Regulations deter individuals from participating in vibrant local communities which have historically managed many lower level risks while fear of a lack of shared social norms (e.g. the probability that an individual's efforts to resolve local issues may be met with abuse or even violence) act as a further disincentive to try to make local communities function. Instead individuals form a client relationship with the state and try to work directly with it to deal with the issues that concern them. Because the central state's *modus operandi* has been one-size-fits-all regulation to deal with the problems of its petitioners, yet more regulation flows, debilitating civil society. [41]

It may of course be that this is part of an evolution in society that should be accepted rather than attacked. Maybe the 21st Century world does not require anything in-between the citizen and the state because advances in governance and technology have made them superfluous. Maybe we simply don't need to know or work with our neighbour any more because EU regulation can solve the issues that naturally arise more effectively than local communities. The evidence I see, though, is that reducing risk through central regulation causes many problems. Furthermore, to the extent that it damages self-reliance and local communities, it is dangerous. It destroys the resilience of our society.

If there is little sense of shared values, which are often nurtured and reinforced in local communities, a much greater proportion of the population will engage in gaming the regulatory system, milking it for what it is worth. Any regulatory system would find this difficult to cope with. Its automatic response is ever more prescriptive regulation to combat gaming and this prescription strengthens the downward spiral of societal decline.

Without healthy communities to check and challenge the excesses of the regulatory state, the client relationship between the citizen and the state is strengthened. It takes a brave or foolish person to question the wisdom of his or her patron. If the educated mass of the population is ill equipped by the experience of regulation to organise and coalesce to oppose specific policies, high quality governance cannot be assured. To be specific, the danger of corruption or tyranny increases.

---

41 For example the parishes of Rogate and Milland which I represent both now want government appointed community wardens to deal with anti social behaviour by local youths. The regulatory state has, in part, made public spirited locals fearful of the consequences of taking local action without reference to government to tackle the problem themselves as would have happened in a previous generation.

As recent historical research has shown,[42] fascism in Italy was far less insidious than it might have been because a complex web of loyalties to extended family, church, region and local patron conspired to frustrate the best efforts of the fascist state to corrupt Italian society. Without such strong communities between the individual and the state, the risk of societal failure is much greater.

Chapter 4
THE EUROPEAN DIMENSION

In the previous chapter, I focused on "the state" without generally seeking to discriminate between the British state and the European Union. We are now in a situation where regulatory powers that were once exercised by the British State have been or are being transferred to the European Union. The Lisbon Treaty lists the following areas in which powers have been transferred:-

Article 2 B

1. The Union shall have exclusive competence in the following areas:

    (a) customs union;

    (b) the establishing of the competition rules necessary
    for the functioning of the internal market;

    (c) monetary policy for the Member States whose currency is the euro;

    (d) the conservation of marine biological resources
    under the common fisheries policy;

    (e) common commercial policy.

2. The Union shall also have exclusive competence for the conclusion of an international agreement when its conclusion is provided for in a legislative act of the Union or is necessary to enable the Union to exercise its internal competence, or insofar as its conclusion may affect common rules or alter their scope.

Article 2 C

2. Shared competence between the Union and the Member States applies in the following principal areas:

---

42   A.J.B. Bosworth: *Mussolini's Italy* (2005)

(a) internal market;

(b) social policy, for the aspects defined in this Treaty;

(c) economic, social and territorial cohesion;

(d) agriculture and fisheries, excluding the conservation of marine biological resources;

(e) environment;

(f) consumer protection;

(g) transport;

(h) trans-European networks;

(i) energy;

(j) area of freedom, security and justice;

(k) common safety concerns in public health matters"[43]

Further to this Article 2 D (2) states that, "The Union shall take measures to ensure coordination of the employment policies of the Member States, in particular by defining guidelines for these policies." Article 2 E states that "The Union shall have competence to carry out actions to support, coordinate or supplement the actions of the Member States. The areas of such action shall, at European level, be:

(a) protection and improvement of human health;

(b) industry;

(c) culture;

(d) tourism;

(e) education, vocational training, youth and sport;

(f) civil protection;

(g) administrative cooperation."[44]

4.1 ARTICLE 308

If this array of competencies proves insufficient, the EU can always turn to Article 308 of the EC Treaty (Nice consolidated version) which states that, "If action by

43   *The Lisbon Treaty*, p. 53 – 54

44   *Ibid*, p. 54 – 55

the Community should prove necessary to attain, in the course of the operation of the common market, one of the objectives of the Community, and this Treaty has not provided the necessary powers, the Council shall, acting unanimously on a proposal from the Commission and after consulting the European Parliament, take appropriate measures." This article to quote the Commission's own legal service,

"has been widely interpreted by the Institutions, in order to cover all purposes and objects coming within the general framework of the Treaty, and not only those listed in Article 3 [list of the objectives of the European Union]. A recent example of this practice is the adoption of the Regulation establishing the Agency on Fundamental Rights."[45]

This clause will remain in the Lisbon Treaty that Mr Brown has accepted on our behalf. Article 308 does, of course, have the safeguard that unanimity at the European Council gives British ministers a veto but, the House of Lords Select Committee on the European Union makes it clear in its report,[46] "there is a danger that any 'flexibility' clause could be used as a way of bypassing the need to amend the Constitution and the parliamentary democratic control and national constitutional requirements that would imply."[47]

The select committee goes on to cast doubt on the value of drawing up a list of competencies such as those set out above when such a catch all/fall back clause is included. Thus we appear to have a situation where the European Union can make laws and regulations on almost any subject. The EU has previously used this flexibility clause to create a Community Trademark; the European Company; a Community action programme in the field of civil protection; and a rapid reaction mechanism for humanitarian aid. Some of these measures may not have been unworthy in themselves. They do, however, suggest a European Commission that is not reticent in the exercise of any powers that are granted to it.

4.2 WHY THE EU OVER-REGULATES

The vast transfer of rights to make laws and regulations furthers several EU-related factors favouring excessive regulation. They include:

---

45 *Opinion of the Legal Service*, European Council, Brussels, 22nd June 2007

46 *The Future of Europe: Constitutional Treaty - Draft Articles 1-16*, HL61, House of Lords, 27th February 2003, para. 82.

47 *Ibid*

1. the drive for harmonisation;

2. the precautionary principle;

3. the lack of a proper cost/benefit analysis;

4. the expansion of the EU;

5. implementation of EU law in the UK;

6. the difficulty of reform and repeal;

7. the division of powers; and

8. the Charter of Fundamental Rights.

Each of these is explored below.

4.2.1 Drive for Harmonisation

The EU prizes common positions for their own sake. For European idealists the common position has become the definition of victory as it signals that the unitary European state they aspire to create has become a bit more real. Given the diverse backgrounds and traditions in the EU, a common position is unlikely to exist without some impetus from the European Commission. More often than not, further regulation is the only means open to the European Commission bureaucrats to move the EU's nations toward a common position. Thus regulation, such as European Directives, otherwise not rationally justified by any cost/benefit analysis is pursued because of the integrationist ideal. As Josef Konvitz, Chief Regulatory Economist of the OECD diplomatically put it, "Consensus based decisions may – mean a relative disregard for the practical evidence of what might work best."[48] Or to quote our former Europhile prime minister, Mr Blair, "It often seems to want to regulate too heavily without sufficient cause".[49]

4.2.2 The Precautionary Principle

In trying to understand the role the precautionary principle has on reducing our exposure to risk through increased regulation, it is helpful to start by understanding the principle and its different interpretations. The precautionary principle was first recognised in the World Charter for Nature, adopted by the UN General Assembly in 1982. There are areas in which references to the precautionary principle may well be warranted – perhaps to protect the environment as set out in the 1992 Rio

48 Speech entitled *The Institutional Context for Better Regulation* (Amsterdam) 7-8th Oct 2004, p. 16

49 Speech to the IPPR – May 2005

Declaration, whose principle 15 states that, "in order to protect the environment, the precautionary approach shall be widely applied by States according to their capability. Where there are threats of serious or irreversible damage, lack of full scientific certainty shall not be used as a reason for postponing cost effective measures to prevent environmental degradation."

Professor Ragnar Lofstedt[50] puts forward three versions of the precautionary principle:

- Version 1: Uncertainty does not justify inaction. In its most basic form, the precautionary principle is a principle that permits regulation in the absence of complete evidence about the particular risk scenario. [Lack of full scientific certainty shall not be used as a reason for postponing measures to prevent environmental degradation – Bergen Declaration.]

- Version 2: Uncertainty justifies action. This version of the precautionary approach is more aggressive.

- Version 3: Uncertainty requires shifting the burden and standard of proof. This version of the precautionary principle is the most aggressive. It holds that uncertain risk requires forbidding the potentially risky activity until the proponent of the activity demonstrates that it poses no (or an acceptable) risk.

Lofstedt argues that the EU's connection with the precautionary principle started with Version 1 (for example with respect to protecting the North Sea from the damaging effects of the most dangerous substances) something few would quarrel with, but that it has, with some variation between different European Commission directorates, progressed towards adopting Version 3. For example, the EU Chemical White Paper of 13th February 2001 sets out to place responsibility on industry to ensure that only chemicals that are safe for the intended purposes are produced and completely reverses the burden of proof for innovators so that the innovator is forced to prove beyond reasonable doubt that a chemical innovation is not harmful. Regulation on such a basis is clearly damaging for a creative society as innovators will be unwilling to take risks developing a product which may be rejected by a regulator on the basis of Lofstedt describes as "excessive emotionalism".[51]

---

50   In section 1 of a paper presented at Merton College, Oxford 5th-11th April 2002. He gives Wiener and
     Rogers credit for the analysis

51   *Ibid* – Section 4

Given that, as discussed above, action under the precautionary principle can be triggered by a very low risk, it provides grounds for widespread regulation of almost every aspect of an area to which is may be held to legitimately apply. Thankfully it only applies to some areas of EU policy. In its, *Communication from the Commission on the Precautionary Principle*[52] the European Commission states that, "The precautionary principle is not defined in the Treaty, which prescribes it only once – to protect the environment. But, in practice, its scope is much wider [covering areas where] effects on the environment, human, animal or plant health may be inconsistent with the high level of protection chosen for the Community."[53] In legal terms, the Commission is justified in taking this approach as to where it can apply the precautionary principle as the European Court of Justice confirmed that it could be used in the May 1998 judgement it issued against the British Government.[54] In that judgment it upheld the European Commission's right to ban British beef, stating that the measure would only be illegal if it had been manifestly inappropriate.

The precautionary principle gives the European Commission stunningly wide powers to take regulatory action in the areas of health and safety, the environment and consumer protection. As Ursula Schiessner points out, Commission action under the precautionary principle is, "subject to limited judicial review only, namely in relation to:-

(i) misuse of powers (e.g. an arbitrary measure);

(ii) manifest error (e.g. wrong facts); or

(iii) exceeding bounds of discretion."[55]

This is not a merely theoretical concern. For example, with regard to the passing of very strict standards for aflatoxins in ground nuts in the name of the precautionary principle by the EU in the late 1990s, World Bank economists took the view that this would lead to a 64% reduction in the export of African crops to the EU, with a monetary worth of $700 million a year, in order to reduce deaths from liver cancer by possibly 1.4 deaths per billion a year.[56]

---

52 Brussels 02.02.2006 COM (2000) 1

53 *Communication from the Commission on the precautionary principle* – (Brussels) 02.02.2006 COM (2000) 1, p. 3

54 Ref: C-180/96

55 Ursula Schliessner of Oppenheimer Wolff and Donnelly LLP of the *International Environmental Law Committee Newsletter*, November 2000, p. 7

56 Cited by Ragnar Lofstedt in section 4 of a paper presented at Merton College, Oxford 5th - 11th April 2002

The Commission acknowledges, in its discussion of the precautionary principle, that, "the decision to do nothing may be a response in its own right."[57] It also states that, "Maintenance of the measures depends on the development of scientific knowledge, in the light of which they should be re-evaluated."[58] This purports to provide some clarity about the extent to which the European Commission will seek to use the precautionary principle to justify regulation. It also sets out that, "recourse to the precautionary principle presupposes:-

- identification of potentially negative effects resulting from a phenomenon, practice or process;

- a scientific evaluation of the risk which because of the insufficiency of the data, their inconclusive or imprecise nature, makes it impossible to determine with sufficient certainty the risk in question."[59]

Given the above, we might be reassured that the European Commission will seek to apply the precautionary principle in a rational and evidence-based manner. Unfortunately we cannot derive much solace from this because:-

- the breadth of the policy areas in which the European Court of Justice has granted the European Commission permission to use the precautionary principle;

- the low intrinsic burden of evidence which it requires to justify regulatory action under the precautionary principle; and the fact that, as the European Commission itself notes, it will seek to apply the precautionary principle on the basis of, "potentially dangerous effects ... inconsistent with the high level of protection chosen for the Community."[60] That is to say that the default level of protection which the European Commission will seek to provide with respect to the precautionary principle is a high rather than a pragmatically moderate or low (in extremis only) level with obvious negative implications for allowing organisations and individuals freedom to act.

---

57 *Communication from the Commission on the precautionary principle* – (Brussels) 02.02.2006 COM (2000) 1, p. 15

58 *Ibid,* p. 21

59 *Ibid,* p. 15

60 *Communication from the Commission on the precautionary principle* – (Brussels) 02.02.2006 COM (2000) 1, p. 3

In combination, the above factors ensure that the precautionary principle, which in several policy areas such as health and safety, may be very broadly drawn, is a major driver of freedom-reducing regulation.

These tendencies are exacerbated by the rather odd way in which the European Courts have interpreted the precautionary principle. In a fascinating study G. Marchant and K. Mossman set out,[61] through detailed analysis of three legal cases, how the European Courts have not interpreted the precautionary principle in a consistent fashion. They highlight two examples applying Version 3 (the most extreme form) of the precautionary principle.

The first example is provided by the *Fornasar* case, in which the European Court of Justice eliminated – on the basis of the precautionary principle – the requirement that the Italian government give fair notice to a company it wished to prosecute for hazardous waste violations. This is not in itself extraordinary. What is extraordinary is that the "hazardous waste" in question did not meet the definition of hazardous waste in either Italian national law or the relevant EU directive. In other words, a prosecution without due notice was permitted by the European Court, on the basis of a very precautionary interpretation of the law by the Italian government which the company in question could not have foreseen.[62]

The second example is the *Virginiamycin* case (Virginiamycin is a form of animal anti-biotic). The European Commission sought a scientific opinion on the risks its use posed to human health from an advisory committee, the Scientific Committee for Animal Nutrition (SCAN). SCAN concluded that there was no immediate risk from Virginiamycin and that there would be no risk from continued use of the antibiotic while further data on its safety was gathered and evaluated. Nevertheless, the Commission and European Council delisted (banned) Virginiamycin and an animal growth promoter (bacitracin) before SCAN completed further work. When this decision was contested at the Court of First Instance, the Court upheld the ban arguing the Commission and Council were entitled to make use of SCAN evidence but, under the precautionary principle, could use that to support a ban – even though that was contrary to what SCAN concluded. The Court agreed with those defending the EU institutions that if the existence of risk could not be excluded (a very low, almost nonexistent standard of proof), there was no need to undertake a quantitative assessment of that risk before taking protective action.[63]

61 *Arbitrary and Capricious – The Precautionary Principle in the European Union Courts* (2005) International Policy Press, Chapter 5

62 Case C-318/98, *Fornasar et al. v. Italy*, 2000 E.C.R. I-4785 (2000) (Celex No. 6980C318), Ruling 1

63 *Pfizer Animal Health SA v. Council* 1999 E.C.R. II-1961

Conversely, France found that the European Courts would not apply the precautionary principle without regard for the requirement for evidence when it claimed that the Commission had violated the precautionary principle by authorising UK beef exports without regard to some possible health risks connected to BSE.[64] Further to this, when the European Commission prosecuted France in the European Court of Justice for refusing to lift the ban on British beef, the Court sided with the Commission and stated that the scientific opinion of its own food safety agency that some risks might remain was insufficient and that the precautionary principle did not oblige the Commission to follow every scientific opinion without the power to carry out its own assessment.[65]

It is noteworthy that the court appears to allow the other European institutions (the Commission and Council) a relatively free rein in using the precautionary principle to justify their decisions, even if it is more demanding of national governments when they oppose the ends the European institutions are seeking.

While we may regard the above series of cases as better than the European Court perpetually interpreting the precautionary principle in its most aggressive form (Version 3) the lack of clarity as to how the law will be interpreted inclines policy implementers and all those organisations and individuals which wish to conduct their activities within the confines of the law to exercise the maximum risk aversion possible with negative consequences for any society that aspires to have the majority within it being relatively free citizens leading fulfilled lives.

4.2.3 Lack of a Proper Cost/Benefit Analysis

British Regulatory Impact Assessments are often flawed documents designed to provide a post hoc justification to policies ministers have already decided on.[66] Thus in the UK the case against a regulation is often not strongly put by those with responsibility for advising ministers.

In the EU the position is often worse. Those who question the need for an EU regulation are often regarded as Europhobes, trying to spoil the EU's agenda of centralisation rather than as valued interlocutors — with a case to make as strong as those who campaign for more regulation.

---

64 Case C-514/99, *French Republic v. Commission* 2000 E.C.R. I-4705

65 Case C-1/00, *Commission v. French Republic* 2001 E.C.R. I-9989

66 National Audit Office - *Evaluation of Regulatory Impact Assessments Compendium Report* 2004-05

4.2.4 Expansion of the EU

The expansion of the EU has created many advantages for the UK, in that it has brought in members who, conscious of the failings of the socialist system in which they were enmeshed for forty years, are less than anxious to see it recreated by the European Union's institutions. That said, the admittance of former Warsaw Pact countries has strengthened the hand of the European Commission because many of the states taken on had inadequate legal systems and structures – something that could not be said, to any great extent, of the fifteen member states that formed the EU prior to 1st May 2004. The European Union has worked hard to ensure that the new member states could endeavour to apply the *acquis communautaire*. To be fair, the process of asking a new state to implement it has also caused the EU to appreciate the incoherence of some of its legislation and to seek to simplify it. That has been a positive development for all states in the European Union although, as discussed further below, meaningful simplification has, to date, been thin on the ground.

The inadequacy, in many cases, of the system of domestic law in accession states has given the European Commission sound intellectual reasons to propose further measures to harmonise laws – namely that doing so should help drive up the standards in the recent accession countries. The problem for the UK with this is twofold:-

- the Anglo-Saxon legal model does not harmonise easily with the system of Roman Law common in continental Europe; and

- whereas many states which were once on the other side of the Iron Curtain may benefit from EU legislation and standards where none existed in the past, we already have our own which are complicated by the over-layering of European legislation.

Thus, on balance, while the accession of new member states may have changed the political dynamic of the EU, it has probably encouraged the European institutions to be more bold in proposing harmonising measures, sure in the knowledge that many countries within the EU could not credibly defend their existing national systems as efficient or effective.

4.2.5 Implementation of EU law in the UK

Having touched upon the issue of implementing European law in new member states it is worth reflecting on the way in which EU law is implemented in the UK and the drivers that this creates for over-regulation. The process with respect to European legislation is that once it has been adopted by the Parliament and Council jointly, each member state must decide how to transpose EU law into national legislation. It must then put in place administrative arrangements to implement and enforce the new law before starting to police the application of the new law and apply suitable sanctions as required.

Further to this there are two principal types of EU law:[67]

- Regulations are directly applicable in English or Scottish law and their requirements do not therefore need to be transposed into domestic legislation. Nevertheless, in the UK some form of so called "top up" legislation is usually necessary, in particular to ensure that effective sanctions are in place.

- Directives are binding on all EU countries to which they are addressed. They set out the result to be achieved but leave to the national authorities the choice of form and methods. They have no effect in the UK until they are transposed into English or Scottish law.[68]

I have set out the details above to make clear the process whereby national authorities become enmeshed in the business of EU law making away from the negotiating tables in Brussels and Strasbourg. The first issue we encounter is one of ambiguity. As the National Audit Office points out in its excellent analysis of the issues connected with implementation, "The UK is now one of 25 [now 27] member states. Alongside the ambiguity which results from the negotiation of a legal text between this number of parties, legislation may embody compromises and, together with differences in language, this may result in uncertainties and gaps in the Regulation or Directive."[69] As William Robinson notes:

> "most harmonising legislation is adopted on the basis of political compromise using the complex and time-consuming co-decision

---

67 *Lost in Translation ? – Responding to the Challenges of EU Law* (NAO) May 2004, p. 11

68 Though the courts can sometimes give a Directive "direct effect" if a Member State fails to transpose it

69 *Lost in Translation ? – Responding to the Challenges of EU Law* (NAO) May 2004, p. 12

procedure, in which none of the institutions or the member states have a determinative role." [70]

Lest the message not be clear about the problematic nature of the EU law that the UK is asked to implement, it is worth quoting a member of the European Commission Legal Service:

"The European Parliament, under the co-decision procedure, is allowed to propose uniformed, irrational, impractical amendments, safe in the knowledge that they have no responsibility for implementation."[71]

This ambiguity is not helped by the fact that the European Commission has no legal power to clarify legislation once it has been adopted. It can, of course, refer cases to the European Court of Justice if it feels that the requirements of a Directive have been breached but the onus is on the member states to arrive at a "correct" interpretation of a European law.

In addition to the ambiguity, there is pressure for national governments to implement measures at speed. The European Commission monitors whether EU countries are meeting deadlines for the transposition of EU law through an Internal Market Scoreboard published annually. A major reason for infringement proceedings is late implementation of a Directive. Because, whilst they rarely result in a fine,[72] infringement proceedings are resource intensive and administratively expensive to deal with, departments seek to avoid them by implementing on time. This is done either by copying out the text of the directive or by elaborating on the directive to give greater clarity and certainty to those affected by it.

This system inclines towards over implementation and hence over regulation of risk (even in terms of the level of protection which the bureaucrats in the Commission originally intended). Organisations, anxious not to break the law, take the most cautious approach possible and over implement a directive because the department concerned has taken a copy-out approach which may make the meaning of the EU law ambiguous. For example with respect to the Large Combustion Plants Directive the copy out approach was used in November 2002 and this led to an increase in questions from industry about what the transposing legislations means.[73]

70 "Bad" EU regulation: prevention and cure, PLC Global Counsel Dispute Resolution 2004/05 written by William Robinson of Freshfields Bruckhaus Deringer, p. 8

71 Quoted on p. 8 of PLC Global Counsel Dispute Resolution 2004/05 written by William Robinson of Freshfields Bruckhaus Deringer who in turn takes the quote from "Implementation of EU legislation. An independent study for the Foreign & Commonwealth Office" by Robin Bellis published in November 2003

72 This may change under the Treaty of Lisbon which may make provision to speed up infringements for non-transposition

73 Lost in Translation ? – Responding to the Challenges of EU Law (NAO) May 2004, p. 25

Alternatively departments are too slow to produce guidance — industry has to make up its own mind and hence takes a cautious approach on the rational grounds that it is commercially cheaper to over-implement once than to under-implement and then face the prospect of having to implement again, possibly after a fine. On the Animal By-Products Regulation, for example, guidance notes were only issued to key industry sectors a year after legislation had come into force.[74]

In seeking to clarify the legislation, a department can itself slip into gold plating by extending the scope of the European law in national law or adding requirements to those in the European legislation. For example, some stakeholders thought that Defra went further than required in its implementation of the Pig Welfare Directives with its "Code of Recommendations for the Welfare of Livestock: Pigs" which is a national initiative and is not a requirement of the Directives. The code contains recommendations that are based on good practice and highlights the latest developments in husbandry techniques. [75]

In comparison with national legislation – where those responsible for creating the legislation also have a hand in clarifying and implementing it – the way in which EU law is implemented is likely to ensure that it is more constrictive than it should be and that it is frequently interpreted in an overly risk adverse way for reasons which make sense to those engaged in transposition but which do society as a whole no favours.

4.2.6 Difficulty of Reform and Repeal

Repealing an Act of Parliament is not exactly easy but substantial amendments can be made relatively easily through the use of another bill or Regulatory Reform Order by a government that enjoys a majority in the House of Commons. It is possible to agree to reform regulations which prove not to work well and to effect rapid change – if need be.

But when a European Directive (such as the Sixth VAT Directive) proves to be deeply flawed, then it is an order of magnitude more difficult to reform because everyone who wishes to reform it is all too aware of the painful international compromises which its original drafting entailed and are even fearful of trying for improvement on the basis that, once a rewriting or repeal process is entered into, the net outcome may be an even worse regulation. For example, what will be a purely pragmatic simplification to someone in a Directorate General at the Commission will be a point of principle for a set of nations at the European Council or a powerful bloc within

74 *Ibid,* p. 6

75 *Ibid,* p. 26

the European Parliament. To be fair, Charlie McCreevy,[76] the EU Commissioner for Internal Markets, has made some effort to roll back the tide of EU regulation but he has been scarcely more successful that King Canute. The dynamics of the European project are such that undoing measures is difficult and this is likely to remain so for so long as the European Commission is regarded by many, including its own staffers, as the principle motor for creating a unitary European state. In such circumstances, repeal or reform smacks of European failure.

In summary, whatever damage the excessive regulatory state has done to our country since 1940, institutional features and the ideology of Europeanism mean that the EU is more predisposed to ill thought out and damaging regulation than the UK and that, when the damage becomes apparent, it is much more difficult to effect change.

4.2.7 Division of Powers

Article 2 A (2) of the Lisbon Treaty states, "Where the Treaties confer on the Union a competence shared with the Member States in a specific area, the Union and the Member States may legislate and adopt legally binding acts in that area. The Member States shall exercise their competence to the extent that the Union has not exercised its competence. The Member States shall again exercise their competence to the extent that the Union has decided to cease exercising its competence."[77] As shown on pages 36-37 a large number of areas are covered by this shared authority. In purely legal terms the sharing may make logical sense but the net effect is to create a significant driver for further legislation:-

- the European Commission and Parliament have vast areas where they can seek to harmonise in pursuit of their consensual European state, despite any national laws which may remain in place. The net result of this is often duplicative sets of regulation which gold plate anything either the EU or the national government sought to create; and

- the national ministries covering these areas of policy are left with some power of initiative in the narrow sub sectors where the EU has not yet seen fit to legislate. Only there may they look for national legislative proposals that will make their ministers appear active. This leads them to consider legislation, for the sake of appearing active and justifying their existence, in areas in which, without the sharing of powers with the EU, they would not seek to legislate. Sharing also provides incentives (as the

76   Cf. His speech to the Legal Affairs Committee of the European Parliament, 2nd February 2005

77   *The Lisbon Treaty*, p. 52

European Commission starts to consider an area currently under national control) for an image conscious minister to regulate – he or she can seek authority through creating new legislation ahead of what he or she thinks the EU may do next in the hope of improving a nation's chances of influencing future European Commission policy.

- In turn, the above dynamics limit the scope for any national government to delegate real power to the region, county, borough or individual – you can't gift what you don't own.

In short, Article 2 creates a competitive environment for legislation that is likely to lead to political and international gamesmanship in favour of creating more regulation. In these circumstances the chances of an objective cost/benefit analysis of the merits of new regulation are much reduced.

4.2.8 Charter of Fundamental Rights

The extent to which the Charter of Fundamental Rights of the EU will be binding on the UK in the event of the Treaty of Lisbon being ratified is hotly debated. It's difficult to give a definitive opinion on whether it will or won't be binding upon the UK. I merely want to point out how it will add to an unhealthy suppression of risk through excessive regulation if the assurances the Foreign and Commonwealth Office claims to have obtained prove imperfect when tested by the European Court of Justice.

The Charter of Fundamental Rights provides not just negative rights (those enunciated by Locke[78] and others such as free speech which guarantee freedoms in many liberal democracies such as the United States) but positive rights which put obligations on others in society to provide goods and services for others. All other things being equal, a culture of positive rights is far more likely to give rise to freedom being abridged by intrusive regulations than negative rights which require the state and others to refrain from doing things.

The sad reality of the EU's Charter of Fundamental Rights is that many of the negative rights (which guarantee freedom) bear so many caveats that they don't offer much guarantee of freedom. For example, Article II 70 proclaims, "Everyone has the right to freedom of thought, conscience and religion."[79] So far, so good. Then comes to the explanatory paragraph the Intergovernmental Conference feels necessary to attach to this right. This states that it may be subject to limitation, "as

---

78 Section 22, Chapter 4 - *Second Treatise of Government* – John Locke (1690)

79 *Conference of the Representative Governments of the Member States – Draft Declarations CIG 3/07* (Brussels) 23rd July 2007, p. 11

are prescribed by law and are necessary in a democratic society in the interests of public safety, for the protection of public order, health or morals, or for the protection of the rights and freedoms of others."[80] Poor calibre indeed would be the bureaucrat, even if he were not to gravitate to the extremes of Robespierre's Committee of Public Safety, if he could not use these limitations so as to make any attempt to uphold such freedom-enhancing rights meaningless when they stood in the way of a risk reducing regulation.

By contrast the Charter of Fundamental Rights enjoins, for example:

- Article II-75: "Everyone has the right to engage in work and to pursue a freely chosen or accepted occupation."[81]

- Article II-89: "Everyone has the right of access to a free placement service."[82]

- Article II-93: "The family shall enjoy economic and social protection."[83]

- Article II-95: "A high level of human health protection shall be ensured in definition and implementation of all the Union's policies and activities."[84]

- Article II- 98: "Union policies shall ensure a high level of consumer protection."[85]

While many of these positive rights are also qualified, to a degree, by the explanatory paragraphs attached to the Intergovernmental Conference declarations this does not undermine the reality that many of them can, and undoubtedly will, provide legal justification for further widespread EU regulation in many fields. For example, the injunction of Article II-83 that, "Equality between women and men must be ensured in all areas, including employment, work and pay"[86] provides legal rationale for the most intrusive regulations in many aspects of men and women's lives as it goes beyond equality of opportunity and makes a theoretical aspiration to precise equality of outcome a right which the state must work to ensure through laws and regulation.

80 *Ibid*, p. 28
81 *Ibid*, p. 12
82 *Ibid*, p. 15
83 *Ibid*, p. 16
84 *Ibid*, p. 17
85 *Ibid*, p. 17
86 *Ibid*, p. 14

To summarise, the Charter of Fundamental Rights, if it is binding on the UK, or even just slightly more influential on European Commission initiatives following the adoption of the new treaty must, due to the numerous positive rights which it enshrines, provide a major impetus for significant quantities of freedom inhibiting regulation.

4.3 COSTS OF EU REGULATION

Having noted some of the threats regulation presents above, it is perhaps worth touching on the cost of regulation. Many of the social costs of regulation – the damage to society that it causes – are intrinsically difficult to measure so the costs mentioned below relate to the estimates which others have made of the costs which regulation imposes on business.

The Better Regulation Task Force estimated[87] that the overall cost of regulation was circa 10% of GDP in 2005 which it equated to a cost of c. £100 billion.

Most authoritative commentators such as the Dutch Government would agree that at least 50% of significant new regulations come from the EU[88] – the percentage is a lot higher in the environmental field and lower in other areas such as criminal justice. This would clearly put the 2005 burden of EU regulation at £50 billion a year.

Alternatively, Open Europe tried to cost regulations from the EU using parliamentary answers and burdens information from the British Chambers of Commerce.[89] It calculated that the cost of EU regulation between 1998 and 2005 alone was £30 billion or 77% of the total UK regulatory burden over that period. Given that it was only looking at a finite period, it appears reasonable to assume that the overall cost of EU regulation, in so much that it can be measured is not likely to be that different from the £50 billion which can be calculated from BRTF and Dutch data.

It should be remembered that most methodologies have difficulty properly accounting for the societal costs this paper focuses attention on, so the real total, in as much as it is possible to put a cost in £ on societal damage, is likely to be much higher.

---

87 BRTF Press Release issued 16th March 2005

88 *Regulation – Less is More* – Better Regulation Task Force, p. 25

89 *Less Regulation – 4 ways to cut the burden of EU red tape* – Open Europe – November 2005, pages 20-27

4.4 SUMMARY

A regulatory response to every risk in our society is not a free good. That regulatory response carries great risks for the whole of society. As highlighted by the quotation from Hobbes at the beginning of this paper, the future is at least as bleak without regulation. There is a need to find a balance that recognises the insidious costs to the community of greater regulatory risk management as well as the supposed gains from any individual piece of regulation. This will be the subject of the next chapter.

Chapter 5
TAKING RISKS FOR A GREATER SOCIETY

If the highly regulated situation outlined in the opening chapters of this paper is not optimal then it is necessary to provide innovative solutions to ensure a general and sustainable move away from supranational and national regulatory solutions. We need to consider what is an appropriate approach to regulation by both the British state and EU and to place hurdles in the way of regulation which may be excessive and change the dynamic of the system.

5.1 HURDLES

In the first instance, policy makers need to understand better the adverse consequences of regulation. Processes such as the Regulatory Impact Assessments (RIA) conducted in the UK can be improved in status — so that they are central to policy making rather than an afterthought – a position criticised in the National Audit Office (NAO) report *Evaluation of Regulatory Impact Assessments Compendium Report 2004-05*); and in quality so they can take proper account of unintended consequences.

Several reforms could usefully be made to ensure that risks are not inappropriately managed through regulation:

- better, more robust, cost/benefit analysis; this should demonstrate that all costs and benefits were considered and that the analysis was quantitatively rigorous;

- a systematic approach to considering unintended consequences of the regulation;

- a focus on implementation costs, regulations don't suddenly work by magic and there should be consideration of the capacity of the regulator(s) to introduce the necessary measures to implement and enforce the legislation;

- offsetting measures, separately setting out how they offset both the policy and administrative costs associated with the new legislation;

- details of which alternatives to classic regulation have been considered and how these might / might not work; and

- details of when the post implementation review was going to take place and whether sun-setting is possible.

Further to this, the state might usefully regulate its own response to tragic accidents and other events by subscribing to a compulsory cooling off period before regulation is enacted in response to a disaster. For example, in the wake of a train crash, ministers would be able to propose legislation but Parliament might introduce a convention of waiting for a year before granting any bill a second reading in either House. This would give time for passions to cool, the need for further regulation to be questioned and its adverse consequences properly understood. This would obviously be challenging and, in the light of the perceived terrorist threat, might not be an absolute rule.

That said, the Government should adopt it as a default as far too much poor quality and ultimately unnecessary or futile risk-reducing legislation is now on the statue book as a knee jerk reaction to tragedies highlighted by the media. The Dangerous Dogs Act and the blanket ban on legal handguns following the Dunblane killings are perhaps two classic examples showing that such action is not the preserve of Labour politicians. A more recent example of this was the suggestion by Tony Cox, of the advisory committee on dangerous substances, that "The land use planning norms around terminals of this sort [Oil terminals such as Buncefield] have got to be tightened up very considerably."[90] Almost automatic support for such views from politicians such as Dr Phyllis Starkey MP (Chairman of the Select Committee shadowing the Office of the Deputy Prime Minister)[91] illustrate the danger that yet more regulation (whose unintended consequences are unconsidered at the time) is all too often threatened as a knee jerk reaction to a low probability event which did not cause any fatalities. The nature of conversations held in the wake of such events should change.

90 Quoted on BBC Website – 22nd December 2005

91 Quoted in Property Week.com 13th January 2006

5.2 APPROACH TO REGULATION

In order for processes such as regulatory impact assessments to be useful, policy makers need some guidance as to what sorts of risk they should be responding to at an individual level. Ultimately much of the guidance must be political as ministers provide strategic input into policy. That said, one guiding principle might usefully be that central government should regulate to reduce risk over which the individual has little influence such as climate change or pollution (assuming regulation would be a proportionate response). Conversely, *individuals should exercise choice over risks that they are intrinsically capable of managing* (such as what they eat, what sort of DIY they do in their own homes, whether their children go on school trips which may be risky etc).

One example is the regulation that forces all those riding motorcycles on public roads to wear helmets. One rationale for this has been that as the state provides healthcare, it has a role in improving road safety to limit demand on health services. I suggest that those who wish to ride motorcycles without helmets should be free to buy health insurance as a *quid pro quo* for not wearing the helmet, so that, in the event of an accident, they are not a burden on the taxpayer. Not wearing a motorcycle helmet does not have any obvious ill effect on anyone else and many motorcyclists would rather kill themselves than end up paralysed from the neck down following a serious accident.[92]

Of course, deciding which category a risk falls into is not always straightforward and the underlying excuse for many regulations is that they determine the risk an individual is allowed to take for himself or herself on the grounds that what he or she does will have a knock-on effect on the state and other citizens. There are always going to be grey areas where the risk an individual takes may have secondary effects and judgement will always be needed – I'm not in the business of drawing a schematic that policy makers can use in lieu of intelligent thought. That said, at a minimum, policy makers' default option should be no regulation when the risk in question is one which a man or woman with an average level of education is capable of managing for him or herself. This needs to be embraced if the drive towards ever more regulation to eliminate risk is to be reversed.

5.2.1 Changing the Dynamic of the Regulatory System

The above principle – a default position against regulation where individuals are capable of managing the risk – and the hurdles such as the RIA which policy

---

92 Health insurance might well be affordable because the costs to the system of coping with a dead rider are small compared with the costs of treating and caring for one paralysed from the neck down

makers could use to formulate better risk based responses are, of course, not enough. The underlying causes of regulation need to be addressed. In order to make it more likely that policy makers will allow individuals to manage more of their own risks much needs to change.

5.2.2 Educational Improvement

The standard of education needs to improve and the general public needs to be given incentives to achieve higher standards. If the average member of the population is semi-literate and incapable of much analytical thought, there is a case for more regulation than if the average member of the population is relatively erudite and capable of a high degree of quasi-rationale thought. A beneficial spiral may exist. If the average person believes that he or she does not need to pay attention in class because the state will manage all risk in his or her life then a valuable practical incentive to learn is lacking. Conversely, if it is more widely understood that education will help you make good risk calls that you must make for yourself, then there will be a greater incentive to learn. This will feed into a higher general level of education that should make policy makers more comfortable about delegating some risk decisions to the individual.

5.2.3 Healthcare Reform

The current system of state funded, state provided healthcare gives the state a significant incentive to minimise health risks for the population. While this has some positive aspects, it undoubtedly leads to a culture in which bureaucrats strive to minimise popular participation (however worthwhile) in activities that might lead to harm. A different sort of system is required to reduce any incentives the state may have to limit risks that individuals naturally control for themselves (e.g. not air pollution or similar). If healthcare were, to a great degree, funded in a different way, then market-based mechanisms rather than central regulation would influence the amount of risk an individual took with far more benign consequences for society. I appreciate that, for reasons of social equity, state funding of healthcare cannot be entirely abolished but this does not mean that a lot more could not be done by creative minds in government and elsewhere to reduce the role of the state (via healthcare provision) as the individual's risk underwriter of first resort.

5.2.4 Making Alternatives the Norm

As set out in The Better Regulation Task Force report *Imaginative Thinking for Better Regulation*, a lot more could be done by the state to improve the quality of life of the population though consumer education which is likely to have far fewer unintended consequences than classic regulation. For example, many people shopping in a supermarket find it difficult to tell what is healthy. Some form of easily understood system on all food to indicate - at a glance - how nutritionally valuable it was likely to be would put consumers in a better position to manage their own health than going down the rather Orwellian road of the state dictating that which we are allowed to eat and drink.

5.2.5 Using Democracy to Tame the Media

Managing pressure from the media on politicians and civil servants is not something to be undertaken lightly. If a free and well-governed society is to exist, the media plays a valuable role in exposing scandal and keeping government accountable. Nevertheless, as highlighted in Chapter 3, the commercial dynamic of the press ensures that it demands regulatory action to eliminate risk in the wake of tragedies when this is not called for. Given the realities of what sells papers this is unlikely to change and it is not realistic to expect media companies to shy away from activities that will increase their profits. That said, some counterbalance to media pressure is clearly needed. Research into public opinion on any given issue may provide the best possible counter to media spin.

Politicians respond to political pressure because they believe the media influences voters and that they will suffer at the ballot box if the press is not appeased. This may be true to some degree though the evidence on this subject is ambiguous – if anything the press panders to voter intentions rather than leading them.[93] If politicians had the ability, in the wake of any given tragedy, to commission voter research to find out what key voters in key parliamentary seats actually thought about an issue and what action (if any) they thought appropriate, politicians would be much better able to resist hyped up demands from the press for ever more regulation – the hypothesis being that most British voters are far more phlegmatic than most members of the fourth estate.

While politicians currently commission research on voter intentions, at present it has to be paid for by political parties rather than the government so it is used

---

93 *The Press and its Influence on British Political Attitudes Under New Labour* by N.T. Gavin (University of Liverpool) and D. Saunders (Essex University) presented at the Political Studies Association Annual Conference at Aberdeen University 5th-7th April 2002, p. 1

sparingly and, on a relatively non-partisan issue, such as rail regulation, it might not be used at all. Much excessive risk management through regulation could be prevented if the government were to commission high quality taxpayer funded research into what key voters thought in the wake of any given tragedy. In order to avoid handling unfair electoral advantage to the incumbent party, the full results of such research would have to be made public so that all political parties could draw on it during the debate on how to react to the tragedy and for policy planning purposes. This measure, more than anything else acceptable in a democratic polity, would help reduce the influence of the press on regulatory policy because it would provide accurate factual information on the issue which often has most influence on ministers' policy choices. A lack of resources currently leads them to guess or look to ill correlated proxies such as the media for guidance on whether to introduce new laws.

5.2.6 Litigation Reform

Many people are deterred from undertaking community activity because of the risk of litigation. As highlighted in the Better Regulation Task Force report *Better Routes to Redress*, the UK may well have a claims culture, even if it lacks a compensation culture. More needs to be done to challenge the notion that you are likely to be wrapped up in litigation as soon as you do anything in the community that may involve risk. There is a case for researching how the law could be reformed to raise the standard of proof required to prove negligence and similar offences so that those in the community feel empowered to act spontaneously in good faith without the deterrence of being easily sued. The law needs to make it easier for the courts to find that an accident took place (e.g. no one was to blame) while reasonable people were acting in good faith. The cult of endlessly searching for a scapegoat in the mistaken belief that accidents don't just happen must end. There may well be a case for having to prove intent to harm or unreasonable neglect before damages are awarded. This would do a great deal to encourage both community activity and individual responsibility for managing risks.

5.2.7 More Equal Funding for Pressure Groups

The membership of and commitment to pressure groups is unlikely to decrease in absolute terms but measures can be taken to reduce their relative power by providing financial incentives or disincentives which facilitate better representation for those with a more holistic outlook. I see two ways in which this could be achieved – either by severely limiting the proportion of a charity's income that could be devoted to lobbying activity or by giving political parties the same tax privileges as charities currently enjoy. For example, charities such as the National Society for the Prevention of Cruelty to Children spend a very large proportion of their income[94] on lobbying rather than meeting need. This income is raised tax-free so 28% extra (or up to 40% in the case of higher rate tax payers) is added to the value of donations and bequests. By contrast political parties, which take a more holistic view of the society they wish to create, are the poor relations. All individual political donations (save bequests) are subject to income tax.

Whether the system is reformed permissively to permit political parties tax deductibility or through stopping charities spending more than say c.10% of total income on campaigning is largely a matter for HM Treasury and depends on affordability. This is, of course, a far from complete solution to the problems of persistent regulatory campaigning outlined in Chapter 3 but it would be a distinct improvement on the status quo where tax exempt lobbyists representing activists are far better resourced than those parties which attempt to reach out to find solutions for the whole of society.

5.2.8 Central Government Should Do Less

Perhaps most controversially, I suggest that central government should do less. By this, I do not necessarily mean that there should necessarily be less public spending to help the disadvantaged in society but rather that there should be fewer ministers and policy makers at a national and supranational level. More risks should be managed at a local or individual level.

In the 2005/6 session of Parliament more than 40 bills were sponsored by more than 100 ministers, supported by c. 200,000[95] policy-making civil servants. This is a far higher level of regulatory activity than can be readily scrutinised by parliament, public, press or other interested parties. Merely as a function of volume, poor regulations that address risks in an inappropriate way are likely to be passed as a result of this regulatory overload. If three or four bills were being passed it would be simple enough for the relevant parliamentary draftsmen to compare notes with one another and ensure that the drafting of the bills fitted with one another and previous legislation. MPs and Peers would also have time to do this. That task becomes markedly harder with 40 bills with silo working by both policy makers and

---

94 38% of NSPCC income (£34 million) was spent on campaigning in 2004. By contrast, political parties fighting every parliamentary seat in the 2005 General Election were banned by law from spending more than £19.4 million

95 2003 Civil Service Statistics (uses approximation by department to determine number of policy making civil servants – actual figure may be a little lower as some departments such as Defra have operational inspectorates while many Department of Work and Pensions staff are operational)

draftsmen almost inevitable. Central government should delegate far more of its regulation to local communities and this delegation should not simply be confined to enforcement, but rather deciding what rules are appropriate to deal with what risks in the first place. In order to make this a reality, there needs to be fewer ministers and civil servants in Whitehall. Ministers and policy making civil servants, for the reasons outlined in Chapter 3, have a tendency to regulate. If there were half as many ministers and half as many civil servants it is likely that there would be less than half as much management of risks affecting the individual through regulation at a central level. Leading politicians obviously need jobs to reward more junior MPs and working Peers. This need could be addressed in one of two ways.

First, it might be addressed by reducing the number of MPs. If the numbers were cut in half their constituencies would be larger but many high calibre politicians would be forced into local government that would be constructive, if local communities are to be given authority to manage more risks.

Alternatively, it could be addressed by increasing the number of executive jobs offered to MPs. At the moment running many large government agencies is the preserve of civil servants but if more MP's could be given meaningful management roles as an alternative route to the Cabinet, it might assuage the desire to be made a minister. This would be unpopular with some officials but it might well be a price worth paying as an alternative to ministerial jobs which are only justified through the creation of regulation.

The reduction in the number of MP's could be accompanied by a root and branch review of policy-making directorates with a view to reducing massively the number of policy making areas government covers – removing the regulatory expertise from Whitehall in areas where the government decides to delegate risk management to the individual.

In the 1960s and 1970s much of British industry was run by the state and the public was told that it had to be that way otherwise the capitalist system would return to the iniquities witnessed in the Great Depression of the 1930s. Experience of removing industry from the control of the centralised state has proved hugely beneficial to the country. This is partly because of the creation of markets and partly because the individuals running the industries have been freed from state regulations on what risks they could take.

Not every aspect of regulation of risk affecting the individual can be governed by a market but, by genuinely giving local control to counties, boroughs and districts there can be innovation — with different levels of risk regulation in different areas creating constructive competition in the same way as the federal system in the US allows for far more regulatory differences than are permitted in the UK.

In some geographic areas, communities may try to do too little or too much but the success of other geographic areas will act as an example, allowing local communities to adapt levels of risk regulation as evidence (rather than theory) emerges as to which is the right level to foster a sense of community. Given different cultures and traditions, different parts of the UK may find different levels of risk management by the local community rather than the individual are appropriate to their circumstances.

Local communities may seem an abstract concept to some but they are only more of an abstract concept than they should be because they are entrusted with so little. They have no authority to manage the risks many of those who live in them face – most decisions being taken centrally in Whitehall.

But there are numerous advantages to decisions about risk being taken at a local level. The more people are involved in making decisions about risk, the more likely they are to understand both the supposed upside and unintended consequences of regulating the risks an individual is exposed to. The decisions they make will have a far more direct effect on them than on the civil servants in Whitehall or the European Commission bureaucrats in Brussels so they are more likely to come to balanced judgements between the risk individuals may be exposed to if there is no regulation and the rewards which may flow from allowing that degree of additional freedom for the individual to manage his or her own risk.

Moreover:

- Delegated risk based regulation will spread the resources of single issue pressure groups more thinly (unless they genuinely represent local people) while increasing popular participation.

- Citizens are more likely to understand decisions made by those they know, or at a minimum, those they can easily talk to - trust in the decisions taken should therefore increase.

- If the wrong decision is taken, it is far easier to reverse it locally than nationally or at an EU level.

- By giving power to local areas more people will feel a stake in society because they will have more ability to influence decisions on the management of individual risk which are important to them, encouraging them to play an active part in both civic and civil society.

Society will be strengthened to the degree people are empowered rather than made clients of a centralised risk manager. Delegating powers to local communities is not a panacea. It will have a powerful effect – reinvigorating them – but there are wider risks (such as global warming) that are better handled at a national or supranational level while there are others (such as motorcycle helmets) which are best left to the individual. It is probably in relation to education, health care and the areas currently administered but not controlled by local authorities such as planning, roads and social care, that there is the greatest potential for delegation of authority to manage risk. Though it may be more difficult to achieve, there is also a case for delegating health and safety legislation to local areas to discourage the belief that people can't do anything in the community because of ill understood but threatening health and safety laws/inspectors/concerns.

The above analysis would not of course be complete without reference to the increasing role that the EU plays in regulating our daily lives. As discussed in Chapter 4, the political dynamic that leads those in Brussels, Luxembourg and Strasbourg to harmonise all the peoples of Europe into some sort of common framework is undoubtedly one of the most, if not the most powerful force for regulation today. It is so damaging because the regulations in question are so often founded on the ideal of the unitary European state rather than based on evidence that there is any real need for them, let alone that the benefits outweigh the costs.

It is not my purpose in this paper to set out precisely how the current relationship between the EU and the UK should be reformed. Learned men and women have, through the Bruges Group and other fora, offered good ideas on how this might best be achieved. Suffice it to say that there must be change — change which restores the primacy of the British Parliament, which restores to it the power to reject initiatives and regulations from the EU at will rather than have the current *de facto* supremacy of unquestionable EU law. Whether a Norwegian solution (within the European Economic Area) or a Swiss solution (outside the EEA with close links) or even a solution which left us in a radically pared down EU would best further our interests as a sovereign nation is perhaps best left to those tasked with such negotiations. Without such a refocusing of our relations with the EU we may as well give up any aspiration we still harbour to be a nation of free, resilient people, lightly governed and free to seek fulfilment, to live rather than to merely exist in some Orwellian super-state.

Chapter 6
CONCLUDING REMARKS

Good and appropriate regulation will remain a challenge in modern post-industrial societies. There are no easy and simple solutions. It is naïve to think that regulation can simply be abolished if the structures that led to the regulation in the first instance are not reformed. Different societies will decide that different levels of regulation to manage risks to the individual are appropriate to them but, if we do not take action to eliminate the drivers of over-regulation, there will be no society left to decide on what level of regulation is appropriate – merely individuals and the state. On the assumption that this is an undesirable state of affairs, we need to act to correct the tendencies of our current system towards over-regulation to remove risks. This doesn't mean a leap towards a culture where life is nasty, brutish and short for most but rather one where all are more closely involved in decision-making (because, at a minimum, all would have more control to manage the risk in their own lives). The centralised state, while retaining a vital role would not dominate in a risk adverse fashion while the often malign regulatory influence of the EU would be markedly reduced.

The solutions proposed here are not the whole answer but, if fully implemented, they would start to reduce the regulatory overhang and give people a sense of control over their own lives, allowing them and the communities they inhabit, to develop and grow. The reform would create hurdles to inhibit improperly considered regulation of risk and change the dynamic of the regulatory system.

Giving up control is never easy for those enmeshed in the business of government but it is surely better to exercise benign influence over many healthy and vibrant communities than iron control over all risks in a monolithic state in which a culture of risk avoidance is destroying much of what makes life worth living.

William Mason
May 2008

Annex - A Glimmer of Hope

Naked streets – handing back responsibility[96]

The issue

The Department for Transport (DfT) and local authorities design and implement safety measures to prevent road accidents from occurring. The basic road markings, lighting, signs and crossings help responsible motorists drive safely. They are often supplemented with traffic calming features such as speed-bumps and chicanes. Accidents still occur regularly. In 2005, there were 271,017 reported accidents on roads in the UK in 2005. 3,201 people were killed. Even though numbers are decreasing, with ever increasing numbers of people and vehicles travelling in the UK, the risk of transport accidents inevitably remains.

The response

In recent years, several local councils in the UK have been testing an innovative Dutch technique to reduce traffic incidents called 'de-cluttering'. In Wiltshire, white centre-lines were removed from the roads in Seend Village – accidents decreased by a third and the average speed reduced by 5%. In Kensington, the High Street has been de-cluttered of devices originally installed to protect pedestrians. Barriers between pedestrian areas and the road have been removed, kerbs have been stripped away from junctions and the number of street signs has been reduced, resulting in a drop in accidents.

The idea originated in the Netherlands, where the concept (called 'naked streets') has been taken even further. Dangerous junctions have been stripped of traffic lights, road signs, directional markers and pedestrian crossings. To the approaching driver such intersections are totally ambiguous, and with nothing to tell drivers what to do they have to figure it out for themselves. As a result, drivers seem to approach it cautiously and with an eye on what everybody else in the vicinity is up to. Supporters of the 'naked streets' concept argue that drivers, pedestrians and cyclists are forced to interact, make eye contact and adapt to the traffic, instead of relying on signs and signals. They are given more responsibility for their actions on the road. Without the conventional rules of the road in place, drivers tend to slow down and develop an understanding of their environment. It may be that road users

---

96 *Risk, Responsibility and Regulation – Whose Risk is it Anyway ?* (October 2006) Better Regulation Commission, p. 34

pay less attention to their surroundings if they feel protected by an array of signs telling them what to do.

Where 'naked streets' have been adopted, accidents have gone down as have average speeds, and as traffic moves more efficiently journey times have decreased. DfT has commissioned research to explore de-cluttering, suitable speed restrictions and how to minimise the environmental impact of traffic signs and street furniture.

Questions this raises

Can we pass any lessons on to other sectors or is this a unique success?

Is the idea of restoring personal responsibility (rather than relying on external authority) one that can be established in other areas?

Select Bibliography

Application of the Precautionary Principle in the European Union – What Will Change - Ursula Schliessner of Oppenheimer Wolff and Donnelly LLP writing in The International Environmental Law Committee Newsletter, November 2000

Arbitary and Capricious – The Precautionary Principle in the European Courts – Gart E. Marchant and Kenneth L. Mossman (2005) International Policy Press

Bad EU regulation: prevention and cure – William Robinson, Freshfields Bruckhaus Deringer – printed in The PLC Global Legal Counsel Dispute Resolution Handbook 2004/5

Better Regulation for Civil Society – Making life easier for those who help others (November 2005) Better Regulation Task Force

Family Law Reform – opportunities taken, wasted and yet to be seized - Dame Butler-Sloss to the Bar Council - December 2005

Future Challenges – Living with Risk – Tony Blair to the Institute for Public Policy Research – 26th May 2005

Get Connected – Effective Engagement in the EU (Sept 2005) Better Regulation Task Force

Lost in Translation – Responding to the challenges of European Law – National Audit Office – May 2005

Make it Simple, Make it Better (Dec 2004) Better Regulation Task Force

Opinion of the Legal Service, European Council 11198/07, Brussels, 22nd June 2007

Regulation – Less is More – Reducing Burdens, Improving Outcomes (March 2005) Better Regulation Task Force

Risk, Responsibility and Regulation – Whose Risk is it Anyway? (October 2006) Better Regulation Commission

Routes to Better Regulation – A Guide to Alternatives to Classic Regulation (Dec 2005) Better Regulation Task Force

Select Committee of the European Union – Ninth Report (House of Lords) 25th February 2003

The Institutional Context for Better Regulation – Josef Konvitz, Amsterdam, 7-8 October 2004

The Precautionary Principle – Prof Ragnar Lofstedt speaking at Merton College, Oxford – 5th-11th April 2002

Use and Abuse of the Precautionary Principle – ISIS submission to the US Advisory Committee on International Economic Policy Biotech. Working Group, 13th July 2000

THE BRUGES GROUP ASSOCIATE MEMBERSHIP

TEL: +44 (0)20 7287 4414 | www.brugesgroup.com/join | info@brugesgroup.com

To join the Bruges Group, complete the following form and send it to the Membership Secretary with your annual subscription fee. This will entitle you to receive our published material for one year. It also helps cover the cost of the numerous Bruges Group meetings to which all Associate Members are invited. **You can also join online, right now, by using your debit or credit card. Please log on to www.brugesgroup.com/join or you can join over the phone by calling 020 7287 4414.**

Minimum Associate Membership Rates for 1 year UK Member £30 ☐ , Europe £45 ☐ , Rest of the world £60 ☐

Optional donation: £10 ☐ £20 ☐ £50 ☐ £100 ☐ £250 ☐ £500 ☐

Other, please specify: ....

If you are able to give more towards our work, we would be very grateful for your support. For the sake of convenience, we urge you to pay by standing order.

YES! I wish to join the Bruges Group

Title: .... Name: ....

Address: ....

.... Postcode: ....

Telephone: ....

Email: ....

BANKERS ORDER Name and full postal address of your Bank or Building Society

.... Bank/Building Society
To: The Manager:...

Address: ....

.... Postcode: ....

Account number: .... Sort code: ....

Please Pay: Barclays Bank Ltd (Sort Code 20-46-73), 6 Clarence St, Kingston-upon-Thames, Surrey KT1 1NY

The sum of £ .... (figures)

Signature: .... Date: ....

to the credit of the Bruges Group A/C No 90211214 forthwith and on the same day in each subsequent year until further notice.

— or —

CHEQUE PAYMENTS I enclose a cheque made payable to the Bruges Group

The sum of £ .... (figures)

Signature: .... Date: ....

— or —

MEMBERSHIP PAYMENT BY CREDIT/DEBIT CARD

Solo ☐ Visa Card ☐ Visa Delta ☐ Visa Electron ☐ Mastercard ☐ JCB ☐ Switch ☐

Card number: ....

Valid from: .... Expiry date: .... Issue number: .... Security code: ....

Card holder's name as it appears on the card (please print): ....

.Address of card holder: ....

.... Postcode: ....

Telephone:..

Email: .... Signature: .... Date: ....

The Bruges Group
www.brugesgroup.com

Please complete this form and return to:
The Membership Secretary, The Bruges Group, 227 Linen Hall, 162-168 Regent St., London W1B 5TB

Honorary President: The Rt. Hon the Baroness Thatcher of Kesteven, LG OM FRS
Vice-President: The Rt. Hon the Lord Lamont of Lerwick **Co-Chairmen:** Dr Brian Hindley & Barry Legg
Director: Robert Oulds MA **Head of Research:** Dr Helen Szamuely **Washington D.C. Representative:** John O'Sullivan, CBE
Founder Chairman: Lord Harris of High Cross **Former Chairmen:** Dr Martin Holmes & Professor Kenneth Minogue